KATE MULVANY is a playwright, screenwriter and actor. Her writing credits include *Derek Drives a Datsun*, *Vaseline Lollies*, *Blood and Bone* (winner of Naked Theatre Company's Write Now! Award), *Naked Ambition* (ABC Radio), *Story Time*, *Embalmer! The Musical* (Old Fitzroy Theatre Company) co-written with Pip Branson, and the musical *Somewhere...* (Q Theatre) co-written with Tim Minchin.

Kate's play *The Danger Age* was developed at the Australian National Playwrights' Conference, shortlisted for the Sydney Theatre Company's Patrick White Award and premiered at Brisbane's La Boite Theatre in 2008. *The Seed* won the 2004 Philip Parsons Award, premiered Downstairs at Belvoir Street by B Sharp, then moved to the upstairs theatre in 2008 before touring nationally in 2009. It was nominated for an AWGIE for Best New Australian Play in 2008. *The Web* was co-produced by Hothouse Theatre and Black Swan State Theatre Company in 2009.

Kate is currently artist in residence at Sydney's Griffin Theatre and is currently working as a writer and actor on several film, television and stage projects in Australia and internationally.

the WEB

CURRENCY PRESS

SYDNEY

CURRENCY PLAYS

First published in 2011
by Currency Press Pty Ltd,
PO Box 2287, Strawberry Hills, NSW, 2012, Australia
enquiries@currency.com.au
www.currency.com.au

NATIONAL LIBRARY OF AUSTRALIA CIP DATA
    Author: Mulvany, Kate.
    Title: The web / Kate Mulvany;
    ISBN: 9780868199115 (pbk.)
    Dewey Number: A822.4

Typeset by Dean Nottle for Currency Press.
Front cover shows (top) Akos Armont as Travis, (lower left) Robin
Goldsworthy as Fred, and (lower right) Amanda Woodhams as Susan in the
2009 Black Swan / HotHouse Theatre production. (Photo: Karen Donnelly).
Cover design by Emma Vine, Currency Press.

Contents

Currency Press acknowledges the Traditional Owners of the Country on which we live and work. We pay our respects to all Aboriginal and Torres Strait Islander Elders, past and present.

For MWNNN

The Web was first produced by Black Swan Theatre Company and HotHouse Theatre at The Butter Factory Theatre, Wodonga, on 2 September 2009 with the following cast:

TRAVIS	Akos Armont
FRED	Robin Goldsworthy
IVY	Susan Prior
SERGEANT TUKOVSKY	Igor Sas
SUSAN	Amanda Woodhams

Director, Marcelle Schmitz
Set and Costume Design, Bryan Woltjen
Lighting Design, Martin Kinnane
Sound Design, Russell Godsmith
Dramaturg, Campion Decent

CHARACTERS

TRAVIS, 16, school student, prefect
FRED, 16, school student
IVY, 35, Fred's mother
SERGEANT TUKOVSKY, police officer
SUSAN, teenage girl

SETTING

Chapman—an Australian country town.

ACT ONE

SCENE ONE

Lights up on an alleyway in an Australian country town. It is daytime. The sun glints across the concrete. Birds sing. Cars hum in the distance.

Two sixteen-year-old boys, TRAVIS *and* FRED, *in private school uniforms, stand across from each other.* TRAVIS *wears a glittering array of prefect badges.*

They see one another. Smile.

They walk slowly across the stage towards each other. Never taking their eyes off the other's face.

They get face to face and smiles broaden. They could almost kiss.

Beat. Then...

FRED *stabs* TRAVIS. *He thrusts the knife into his stomach deep and hard and holds it there.*

Lower left side of the abdomen.

Their faces still close, TRAVIS *smiles.*

TRAVIS: I love you.

> *He slides off the knife and collapses to the ground.*

> FRED *gets a mobile phone out of* TRAVIS' *pocket. He sits on the pavement, a little way away from the dying* TRAVIS. *He dials the phone.*

FRED: Hello. My name's Fred. I'd like to report a murder.

> *He hangs up, puts the phone back in* TRAVIS' *pocket and waits.*

SCENE TWO

TRAVIS *lies in the same position, only now he is wearing a hospital gown. He gets up, dusts himself off. Smiles at the audience.*

He is bright, chirpy, engaging. Our friend.

TRAVIS: Accidents happen in a town like Chapman.

This hospital caters for the dozen or so towns and stations that are found in the Chapman area. A region of industries where the desert meets the sea. Mining, farming, fishing.

People blow in and out of Chapman with the seasons. Some stay on, settle down. Some of them take off 'cause of the weather, the boredom. But us farming families, we're here to stay. It's all we know.

I'm Travis. I go to St Isidore's College. It's a big school. Nine hundred and fifty pupils. Some boys. Some men. I'll let you decide which category I fit into. Assembly is a sea of long socks and dirty fingernails. It's exam time right now, and despite being in here—or rather, especially because I'm in here—it's all looking pretty good for me.

This is the intensive care ward of Sacred Heart Hospital. They usually deal with farmers crushed by hay bales. Fishermen left fingerless by craypot ropes. Homebirths gone wrong.

Every accident is based around work and family. So you can imagine how exciting it was when I came in. A stabbing. Even though I was in and out of consciousness I could hear the whispers dancing in and out of my head.

A stabbing! A stabbing! He's been stabbed! A stab wound! The nurses went nuts.

The best thing about the word 'stab' is that it sounds like what it is. Stab. Stab. Stab. It's violent but quick. Great letter groupings. The S and the T combine to form a sharp strike that cuts through the A to the B's bite. It's onomatopoeic. Stab. You can see I'll be totally okay with my English exam.

Small towns also attract strangeness. Mystery. Like the girls. The missing girls? Three in four months and not a scrap of evidence. One a Swedish hitchhiker, one a working girl from down the docks and one a barmaid from the local. Gone, just like that. Poor things.

It's left us all in a weird kind of limbo. No-one quite trusts each other. We look at each other differently. 'Is that the guy?' 'Will she be next?' Everyone condemning each other under a big Chapman magnifying glass.

Watching and judging.

We should be kinder to each other, us humans.

He smiles, embarrassed.

Sorry. That was the morphine talking.

Beat.

It's a strange thing, to be stabbed. I didn't even know he'd done it. I didn't even know.

While I was looking into his face, I felt the warm spread of hot fluid on my belly.

But I didn't look down. I was lost in his eyes.

I could smell his breath. I'd never really smelt his breath before. He'd been drinking choc milk. A few hours before, I reckon. A bit sour. But still sweet. And definitely choc milk. Strawberry.

And then I felt him leaving me. I felt that sharp sheath exiting my body. I didn't want it to leave. It felt like it was taking me with it. And then, as my brain filled my body with a potent blend of defensive chemicals… he was gone.

SCENE THREE

FRED *and* SERGEANT TUKOVSKY *sit in an interview room.*

FRED *is covered in blood.*

TUKOVSKY: Can I get you a drink? A water? Cup of tea?

FRED: Can I have anything?

TUKOVSKY: Well, within reason.

FRED: What's within reason?

TUKOVSKY: It means you can't have beer, bourbon, scotch on the rocks or sake.

FRED *looks confused.*

FRED: I just want a choc milk.

TUKOVSKY: A choc milk? I'm sure we can track one down for you. [*He calls out.*] Thommo! Get a choc milk for the interview room, would you?!

FRED: Strawberry choc. Not chocolate choc.

TUKOVSKY: Goes without saying. Strawberry choc, Thommo! [*He gets out a dictaphone and analyses it closely.*] That's 'record', yeah?

FRED *looks. Nods.*

Writing's too bloody small. [*He presses it.*] Try to talk into the bit with the holes.

FRED: 'Kay.

TUKOVSKY: Now, Fred, for the record, could I get you to state your full name, age and place of residence?

FRED: Fred Finch. Sixteen. Lot 23, Rifle Range Road, Rural Mail Box 41, Murchison Flats.

Is Mum okay? Has anyone seen her?

TUKOVSKY: Your mum will be here soon. She was on her way in to work and had to find someone to stay with your sister.

We're going to organise somewhere for you to go. But I need to speak to you about a few things first.

FRED: But is she okay? Mum?

TUKOVSKY: As well as can be expected, Fred. You'll see her soon. She's coming.

FRED: To take me home?

TUKOVSKY: No, Fred mate. You won't be going home.

FRED: I thought I'd be okay. She said you'd make sure I was okay.

TUKOVSKY: She?

FRED: Oh, bum.

TUKOVSKY: You're okay, Fred. Just sit tight. [*Beat.*] You do realise what you've done, mate?

FRED: Yeah. [*He smiles genuinely at* TUKOVSKY.] I'd really like my choc milk.

TUKOVSKY: You stabbed someone, Fred. Travis Masters. Stabbed him right in the gut like a fish.

FRED: I know. [*Beat.*] I didn't want to do it like that. That's not the right way. Gutting them while they're still trying to catch their breath. On the farm it's either a bullet in the head or a cut throat. Quick, easy and painless. I don't think it's right the way the fishermen do it. Dad didn't think so either. But that's how I did it to Trav.

He goes quiet.

TUKOVSKY: How many head you got out there now, Fred? Since…

FRED: Not many. Mum's thinking of selling up. She wants to keep the chooks though. She likes the chooks.

Beat.

TUKOVSKY: I'm gonna need to ask you some questions about why you did it. Understand?

FRED: Is he dead?

TUKOVSKY: No, mate. Not quite. You did some damage though. He's not out of the woods yet.

FRED: So I didn't do it? I didn't kill him?

TUKOVSKY: No.

FRED *gets up and starts pacing.*

FRED: Oh, bum. Oh, bum. Oh, bum…

TUKOVSKY: Sit down please, Fred mate.

FRED: Where's Becky?

TUKOVSKY: She's safe. She's at Mrs Haigh's.

FRED: Are you sure? He hasn't been near her? Have you even checked?

TUKOVSKY: Mate, she's fine.

FRED *keep pacing and moaning.*

FRED: He's not dead? Bum, bum, bum, bum, bum… Where is he?

TUKOVSKY: Hospital. Fred, you're gonna have to sit down or I'll have to handcuff you to the chair, alright?

FRED: I should've known he wasn't dead. He looked different to how Dad looked. Dad was so still. You remember, Sergeant Tukovsky?

TUKOVSKY: I remember, mate.

FRED: Remember how still he was? Like something had just left him. Even the rope wasn't moving.

TUKOVSKY: He'd been in that tree a while, mate.

FRED: But he looked peaceful, didn't he? More peaceful than I'd ever seen him ever.

TUKOVSKY *stares at him.*

Travis isn't dead.

TUKOVSKY: No.

FRED *sits at the table again. He is suddenly calm.*

FRED: How are the other cases going?

TUKOVSKY: What other cases?

FRED: The girls. Susan and the others.

TUKOVSKY: Susan and the others? The missing girls? Is that who you're talking about?

FRED: So you do know them.

TUKOVSKY: Not Susan. But I know of the others. I'm involved in the… investigation.

FRED: How involved? Are you in charge?

TUKOVSKY: Well, no. It's become a state case. I'm pretty high up though.

FRED: But you're not in charge.

TUKOVSKY: Well, I was, but… Fred… these girls you're talking about. The missing ones.

FRED: They're dead. The girls. They're all dead.

TUKOVSKY: You think they've been murdered?

FRED: I know they've been murdered.

TUKOVSKY: You know what happened to them?

FRED: No wonder they took the case off you. [*He leans in close to the dictaphone.*] You're useless.

> *He smiles at* TUKOVSKY.

TUKOVSKY: And what about young Travis Masters? The accident this morning.

FRED: It wasn't an accident. I just fucked up.

TUKOVSKY: Be careful what you say here, Fred.

FRED: Stuffed up. Sorry.

TUKOVSKY: Let's just call it an accident for now.

FRED: It wasn't an accident. He should be dead.

TUKOVSKY: And why should he be dead?

FRED: Because that's what he deserves.

> *Beat.*

TUKOVSKY: I'll get you your choc milk.

FRED: Strawberry.

TUKOVSKY: Yep.

> *He leaves.* FRED *notices the blood on his hands.*
>
> *Lights out.*

SCENE FOUR

A school assembly. TRAVIS *is giving a speech.*

TRAVIS: It is an honour to be elected by both staff and students as head boy of St Isidore's College, Chapman. I commit myself to serving all students, both day and boarding, and maintaining the high standards that are expected from our school and its outstanding scholars. It is also humbling and an unexpected surprise to be elected as not only head prefect, but as captain of Nazareth House as my father was so many years ago. I wish he could be here to see this. It is an honour to take possession of the Prefect Key that he himself would have held tightly. [*He holds a key high.*] I will endeavour to make my parents proud in this, my final year, and thank them for all their love and support. Oh, and carn Wests!

Cheering.

SCENE FIVE

FRED *and* TRAVIS *sit side-by-side at the school gates. The sounds of schoolboys.*

TRAVIS *is on his mobile phone.*

TRAVIS: Yep. I'll see you there around eight… Yeah, it's gonna go off… Righto, mate. See you soon… Remember your ID.

> *He hangs up. Swaps his hands-free for his iPod. Watches the screen, humming.* FRED *watches him, shyly.*

> *After a while,* TRAVIS *notices the boy next to him. Shows him the screen.* FRED *watches.*

Beyonce.
FRED: Huh?

> TRAVIS *takes out one of his earphones. Sticks it in* FRED's *ear.*

> *They sit and listen and watch. After a while,* TRAVIS *takes his earphone out and watches* FRED.

TRAVIS: Fred, yeah?
FRED: [*yelling*] Yeah!
TRAVIS: You're in my Social Studies class, right?
FRED: Yep.
TRAVIS: How'd you go on that test last week?
FRED: Failed it.
TRAVIS: Whoops. Sorry, mate. [*Beat.*] I'm Travis.
FRED: I know.
TRAVIS: You a boarder?

FRED: No.

TRAVIS: You're not a townie, are you?

FRED: [*offended*] No!

TRAVIS: Well, you gotta be one or the other.

FRED: I live on a farm just out of town!

TRAVIS: What family?

FRED: Finch!

TRAVIS: Finch? Out on Rifle Range Road?

FRED *nods, iPod still blaring.*

Isn't your dad the guy who…? Didn't he…?

FRED: [*yelling over the iPod*] Hang himself. Yeah.

TRAVIS *gently removes the earphone from* FRED's *ear.*

Yep. That was my dad.

TRAVIS *smiles gently.*

TRAVIS: I know. [*Beat.*] Sorry. Just wanted to talk to you. I've watched you. You don't say much. [*Beat.*] Why don't you board if you're from a farm?

FRED *doesn't answer. They sit in silence for a while. Then…*

FRED: Mum prefers me to stay out there.

TRAVIS: Fair enough. Bit expensive too, hey?

FRED: Bit.

TRAVIS: Any brothers or sisters?

FRED: Little sister. Becky. She's twelve.

TRAVIS: I heard it was you that found him.

FRED: What?

TRAVIS: Your dad.

FRED *says nothing.*

I just want to make sure you're okay.

Beat. FRED *looks uncomfortable.*

My dad's dead too.

FRED: No he's not. Your dad runs Longfield Station. James Masters.

TRAVIS: He's not my dad. He's my stepdad. And he runs Longfield, Figwood and Tangle Tree Stations, but that's not relevant. He's not my dad.

FRED: What happened to your dad?

TRAVIS: He died when I was twelve. Before I moved here. Accident with the tractor.

FRED: Wow.

TRAVIS: We were ploughing and I was sitting up in the tractor with him and he just fell out. One minute he was there, the next he was wrapped round the wheel. I tried to switch off the engine but we'd gone about a hundred metres before I could work out how to stop it. He'd never shown me, you see. He should've taken the time to show me.

FRED: I didn't know that. I'm sorry.

TRAVIS: A year later Mum married his best mate. James Masters. My stepdad. Then they sent me here.

FRED: Lucky you.

Beat.

TRAVIS: Where do you sit?

FRED: Huh?

TRAVIS: Where do you sit?

FRED: On the farm?

TRAVIS: No. Here. At lunchtime.

FRED: I go to the library.

Beat. TRAVIS *stares at him.*

They've got computers. I sit at the computers.

TRAVIS: Don't you have one on your farm?

FRED: Yeah. We're not that broke. It's old, but it works. I like computers. Games.

TRAVIS: What's your favourite game?

FRED: FIFA 2002. [*Beat.*] I took on Beckham at lunchtime today. He couldn't get it past me.

TRAVIS: Nice work, Freddy! Bet your dad would've been proud.

FRED *goes quiet again. Goes back to the iPod.*

TRAVIS *looks awkward, taps him on the shoulder.*

FRED *takes the earphones out.*

You got internet connection out there?

FRED: Sometimes.

TRAVIS: You on Facebook?

FRED: Nup.

TRAVIS: Myspace?

FRED: No.

TRAVIS: Twitter?

FRED: Uh-uh.

TRAVIS: Bebo?

> FRED *shakes his head.*

They're easy to set up.

FRED: I wouldn't know what to do with one.

TRAVIS: Blog.

FRED: Blog?

TRAVIS: Say stuff. About your life. What you think. What you like. Like a diary that everyone can read.

> FRED *is watching Beyonce again.*

God, you'd think you'd never laid eyes on a woman before. She's not that hot. You going to the party down at the beach tonight?

FRED: Nuh.

TRAVIS: Why not?

FRED: Didn't know about it.

TRAVIS: How could you not know about it? Everyone's going! Well, hopefully. Dunno how many girls will show up.

Since those chicks went missing the private school girls aren't allowed to do anything anymore, but I reckon some girls from St Catherine's will sneak out. Gonna go off. You should come.

FRED: I can't. Babysitting Becky. Mum's gotta work.

TRAVIS: Where does she work?

> FRED *is hesitant.*

FRED: Just part-time.

TRAVIS: Where?

FRED: In town.

TRAVIS: Where?

FRED: IGA. She stacks shelves at night. Only part-time, though. So I've gotta babysit Becky.

> *Beat.*

TRAVIS: You should come and sit with my group one day.

FRED: Why?

TRAVIS: You should extend your social group beyond pixelated soccer players and your little sister.

FRED: I'm alright.

TRAVIS: You'd like my group. They're cool.

FRED: I know.

TRAVIS: Leon's an awesome surfer. Made the semi-pros at Bells last year. Todd's dad owns the biggest station in the southern hemisphere. And Thommo… well, Thommo's a wanker but he has a crop on his property so we put up with him.

FRED: What kind of crop?

TRAVIS grins.

TRAVIS: A really, really green one.

FRED gets it.

Not that I advocate drug use. If it's not your thing, it's not your thing. That's on my Myspace.

FRED: I don't think I have anything to offer your group. Don't have any crops anymore. No stock either.

He glances at TRAVIS nervously.

TRAVIS: What's your email?

FRED: Huh?

TRAVIS: Your email address. You must have an email address. Everyone in the world's got one of them.

FRED: Yeah, I've got one.

TRAVIS: Can I have it?

He gets out a piece of paper and a pen and holds them out to FRED. He doesn't take them.

Can't you remember it?

FRED: Yeah…

TRAVIS: Look, I understand if you don't want to hang out with me and my mates at school. It'd be weird for you and, to be honest, they are a bunch of complete tools. Cool. But tools. But we can at least chat online. Me and you. If you like. [*Beat.*] I could help you with your Social Studies.

FRED: Social Studies? You've never even spoken to me in three years.

TRAVIS: I could say the same thing about you.

> *Beat.* FRED *hesitates.*

> Look... [*He writes on a piece of paper.*] My Myspace. Take a look, see what you think, if you think I'm worth it, let me know.

> FRED *takes the paper.*

> You're a fussy bugger, aren't you?

> TRAVIS *hands back the iPod.*

> You can hold onto the iPod for a few days if you like. There's plenty of Beyonce on there and a little bit of porn in the documentary section. Just give it back to me when you're done.

> FRED *takes the iPod back.* TRAVIS *gets up to leave.*

> See you later, Fred. It was really good to hear your voice.

> *As* TRAVIS *leaves...*

FRED: He was floating.

> TRAVIS *turns to look at him.*

> Dad. He just looked like he was floating.

> TRAVIS *smiles.*

> *Lights down.*

SCENE SIX

TRAVIS *in the hospital.*

TRAVIS: When I was a kid, my parents went away—again—on some overseas trip. Zambia or Zaire... one of those places. It was school holidays, but Mum said I should probably stay here. She told me she didn't want me to get eaten by any lions. That they might mistake me for a little lamb and devour me whole.

So I stayed back in Australia at the primary school boarding house. I spent the days playing basketball in the quadrangle by myself, doing laps of the pool, eating breakfast, lunch and dinner with the brothers. Sleeping alone, in the dark, in a dorm filled with empty bunks and creaking walls...

Until, a few weeks into my holiday, I discovered the unlocked door to the library.

For one long summer, I had that building all to myself. Those books were my only friends and I devoured them whole. One particularly slow week, I pulled out a dusty spine that read *Social Experiments*. It was filled with case studies and scientific scenarios, full to the brim with characters like lab-coated professors and shaved monkeys and isolated orphans. I read it front to back and then started again. I never took that book back. To this day, it's the only thing I've ever stolen and I knew it off by heart by the time I saw my parents again. I'd also grown four inches.

Locked away in that boarding house by myself, reading about the different ways humans will condition each other in order to understand the human condition made those big African lions seem like bunny rabbits and my parents seem... well, unfortunately, human.

He clears his throat.

Case study one: Little Albert.

Professor John Watson hand-picked nine-month-old Little Albert from an orphanage because staff assured him the child was easygoing and happy and rarely cried. This was proven when Watson presented the child with a variety of objects—a rabbit, a dog, a monkey and cotton wool. At no time did Little Albert show any fear. Instead, he quite happily played with all objects.

Later, the child was again presented with the rabbit. This time, as Little Albert went to touch it, Professor Watson banged a gong loudly. Understandably, Little Albert was upset. Watson repeated the gong several times. He then removed the rabbit altogether.

The next time the rabbit was presented to Little Albert he cried immediately and started to move away, despite there being no loud gong. The same thing happened with anything furry or anything white—a monkey, some cotton wool, a Santa Claus mask.

The Little Albert experiment, although cruel, is an example of classical conditioning through fear-mongering. Unfortunately, Little Albert got adopted out before Watson had a chance to recondition him out of his responses to white, fluffy animals. No-one ever found out where he went. It's a pretty safe bet he's not anywhere around here, though. Don't know how he'd go with all the sheep...

SCENE SEVEN

FRED *sits at his computer. The iPod in front of him.*

He reads the piece of paper TRAVIS *gave him and goes to type in the address.*

As he does…

IVY: [*offstage*] Freddo Frog!

> FRED *leaps in fright.*

> IVY *enters.*

Made you jump!

FRED: Mum that stopped being funny about twelve years ago.

> *She gives him a hug and a kiss.*

IVY: Whatcha doin'?

FRED: Nothing.

IVY: Playing games?

FRED: No.

IVY: What's that?

FRED: [*rolling his eyes*] An iPod.

IVY: Yeah?

> *He shows her.*

God almighty. Who's that?

FRED: Beyonce, Mum.

IVY: Is that how you lot dance these days?

FRED: Apparently. Give it back.

IVY: No, no, I like it.

> *She dances around the room, listening to Beyonce and watching the iPod.* FRED *grins.*

Still got it, Freddo Frog.

> *He laughs at her. She looks again at the iPod.*

FRED: Mum!

IVY: Where'd you get it?

FRED: Someone lent it to me.

IVY: Who?

FRED: Someone.

IVY: A girl?

FRED: No.

IVY: Then who?

FRED: Just someone from school. A…

IVY: A…?

FRED: Friend.

IVY: Oh. That's nice. [*She grins to herself.*] Good.

> *She gives him a kiss on the head.*

How'd you go on that Social Studies exam?

> FRED *gets it out. Gives it to her.*

FRED: Sorry.

IVY: Oh, Freddo. What happened?

FRED: I tried, Mum. I really did.

IVY: Did you study for it?

FRED: I tried. The headmaster asked me to give you this…

> *He gives her another letter.*

They reckon you should maybe put me in another school.

IVY: Do they just? Not good enough for them, are we?

FRED: St Isidore's is an agricultural school, Mum. It's for farmers.

IVY: What the bloody hell do they think we are?

FRED: This is a big empty paddock, Mum. Maybe it's time I left school anyway. No point.

> *Beat.*

IVY: I pay your fees, Fred. They can't kick you out and no child of mine is dropping out of school. You deserve a good education. It makes for a good farmer. A great farm. It's what your dad would've wanted. So there'll be no more talk of dropping out, thank you. If I have to I'll pay Mrs Haigh to babysit Becky and I'll get you a tutor.

> *She screws up the letter and places it next to* FRED.

FRED: I don't need a tutor.

IVY: I'm getting you one. You fail one more exam and they're kicking you out. I won't let them do it.

FRED: I've got a friend. At school. He said he'd help.

IVY: He did? What—iPod friend?

> FRED *nods.*

> He any good?

FRED: At everything.

> *Beat.*

IVY: Alright. Good. Use your friend. You're not stupid. Don't give them the satisfaction of shaking their heads at us again, you hear me? We've been here too long. We deserve some respect. Time to wash the shit off ourselves.

> FRED *nods.*

Do your homework. Dinner's in the oven. I'm off.

FRED: 'Bye, Mum.

IVY: Get Miss Muffet in bed by ten. Don't let her give you any grief.

FRED: No, Mum.

IVY: Love you.

FRED: Yes, Mum. Be careful. Park as close to the shop as you can and don't talk to anyone weird.

> *She goes to leave and then stops at the door.* FRED *goes back to the computer.*

Hey, Freddo…

> *He looks up at her as she booties again, à la Beyonce.*

> FRED *throws the screwed-up letter at her.*

> *She goes.*

> FRED *looks again at the piece of paper Travis gave him and types in an address.*

> *Waits a moment. Then reads…*

Travmaster.
Status:

> *Across the stage…* TRAVIS.

TRAVIS: Single.

FRED: Here for:

TRAVIS: Friends, networking, socialising.

FRED: Orientation:

TRAVIS: Straight.

FRED: Home Town:

TRAVIS: Born in Melbourne. Raised all over. Now call Nazareth House, Chapman, home.

FRED: Body Type:

TRAVIS: Six foot. Athletic.

FRED: Smoke:

TRAVIS: Never.

FRED: Drink:

TRAVIS: Yes.

FRED: Drugs:

TRAVIS: It's a personal choice.

FRED: Ethnicity:

TRAVIS: Quarter Scottish, quarter Irish, half English, therefore one hundred per cent Aussie.

FRED: Religion:

TRAVIS: Catholic. Roman.

FRED: Star Sign:

TRAVIS: Virgo.

FRED: Children:

TRAVIS: Not that I know of. LOL.

FRED: 'Lol'? Education:

TRAVIS: Agricultural School. Chapman.

FRED: Occupation:

TRAVIS: Farmer of the future.

FRED: My Blog:

TRAVIS: Hey all… Welcome. For those of you new to my world (and you know who you are) I'm glad you've taken the time.

FRED: 'Since my last blog, a few things have happened.'

TRAVIS: Won hockey championships in the city.

Got an A in my History exam—Nazism. Nothing like Eichmann to make you follow orders. So far maintaining an A average, although Social Studies will be the real doozey. Fingers crossed.

Oh, and got elected head prefect of the school. Got the magic key. A leisure room to myself. Plasma TV, DVD, a Mac, two PCs and a coffee machine.

FRED: Lucky bastard. 'Speech went well, but the brothers had censored a fair bit of what I wanted to say. Don't know why—there was nothing offensive. So here's what I really should have said. Take from it what you will, but I mean every word.'

TRAVIS: There's a certain politics to ag schools that differs to regulation city schools. We slaughter runts and mend tractor engines. Their biggest choice day to day is whether to have a pie or a sausage roll from the canteen. Our families have battled the thirst, the drenchings, the disease of this land. Us boys at this ag school are from the families that won. That took any demon extreme on and beat it into the soil.

Now each generation in our town is being born bigger, stronger, genetically resilient.

Women here don't give birth anymore. They split in two and shove out each massive newborn. But they heal fast 'cause they've improved too. Strong women. Strong men. Strong kids. It's all part of a big tough web.

As head prefect of this fine school, I will do my utmost to ensure we are all part of the same team. Building the same web. Fisherman or farmer, townsperson or boarder.

We are brothers and proudly so.

FRED *gets up from the computer. Goes to the mirror. Looks at himself—pale, scrawny, weak. He flexes his muscles, puffs himself up, but is only embarrassed by what he sees.*

FRED: Stupid runt.

He goes back to the computer. Looks hesitant. Then starts to type…

Hello, Travis. Fred Finch here. Did you still want to help me with Social Studies?

SCENE EIGHT

The police station.

IVY *stands with* SERGEANT TUKOVSKY. *There is an awkward silence.*

TUKOVSKY: Come in.

She looks at him.

Um. Sit down.

He runs to a chair and pulls it up for her. There is a moment of awkwardness as he accidentally almost pulls it out from under her.

Sorry, Ive.

IVY *takes a seat. She is drawn and exhausted.*

/Cuppa?

IVY: /Where is he? /No.

TUKOVSKY: /Safe. Doctors are looking him over.

IVY: Is he hurt?

TUKOVSKY: Not a scratch. He'll be back in a jiff.

IVY: I want to see him now.

TUKOVSKY: You'll see him soon. I promise.

> *Beat.*

IVY: What the hell's going on?

TUKOVSKY: I don't know, Ive. I'm as lost as the rest of the town.

IVY: It's already on the radio.

TUKOVSKY: They haven't named him. They're not allowed to.

IVY: For Christ's sake, Barry, if someone farts in the middle of a paddock at dawn in this town they'll hear it on the docks by breakfast.

> TUKOVSKY *laughs a little too heartily.*

Or have you forgotten the way people talk around here?

> *He stops laughing abruptly.*

They all know who he is. [*Beat.*] Did he do it, Barry? Did he stab Travis?

TUKOVSKY: He's confessed, Ive. I'm waiting to view some security footage from the pub—they have a camera fixed on that back alley for when the bikies hit town—but... he's confessed. Hell, he even called the police.

IVY: Is he alright? Travis. How bad is he?

TUKOVSKY: At this stage, he's still unconscious so we can't know for sure. But it's looking good. Hardly any damage. If there's a place you want to get stabbed, that's where the blade got him.

IVY: Well, what lovely news.

> *Beat.*

TUKOVSKY: He's in the hospital.

IVY: Which one?

TUKOVSKY: I'm afraid I can't tell you that.

IVY: There's only two, Barry. Public and private. It's not gonna be hard to find out.

TUKOVSKY: Confidential. For his own protection.

IVY: I'm not going to go there…

TUKOVSKY: I can't tell you, Ive.

IVY: I only want to send him a card. His poor family…

> *Beat.*

TUKOVSKY: They're not actually here yet. We're trying to track them down. They're somewhere on the Amalfi Coast. Where's that?

IVY: No idea. Sounds nice, though. [*Beat.*] Why would he stab Travis Masters? They're friends.

TUKOVSKY: Are you sure?

IVY: He's been to my house, for God's sake!

TUKOVSKY: When? What for?

IVY: To visit Fred. Help him with his homework. Hang out with him.

TUKOVSKY: You have to admit it's an unlikely friendship. Travis is a top student, sportsman, head boy, and Fred's,, Fred's the kid who…

IVY: Whose father hanged himself from a tree.

> *Beat.*

TUKOVSKY: Has he made any mention of the missing girls to you at all, Ivy?

IVY: No. What have they got to do with anything?

TUKOVSKY: Just something he said.

IVY: I think I'd notice if some missing girls popped up in his bedroom, don't you think, Barry? Don't try to pin that on him too.

TUKOVSKY: He on any medication, Ive?

IVY: What? No!

TUKOVSKY: Drugs?

IVY: He's a good boy. You know that. He wouldn't dare.

TUKOVSKY: Just need to be sure.

IVY: I want to see him.

TUKOVSKY: Soon. I just need to ask you a few more questions.

IVY: Then I want a lawyer present.

TUKOVSKY *looks hurt.*

The whole town's gonna turn on him, Barry. I need to make sure he's alright.

TUKOVSKY: Ive…

IVY: I want a lawyer. Don't call me Ive.

Beat.

TUKOVSKY: You right to sort that out?

IVY: Lawyers? Oh, yeah, I've got a biscuit barrel full of them back at the farm. Jim hadn't even been cut down before they started sliding their cards under the door. Remember?

Beat.

TUKOVSKY: I'll get you one, Ivy. A good one. Not the ones in the biscuit barrel.

Beat.

IVY: Just sort this thing out, Barry. Please. You know us. You know Fred.

TUKOVSKY: I'll do all I can. I promise.

IVY: Now please let me see my little boy.

SCENE NINE

TRAVIS *in hospital.*

TRAVIS: Case study two: The Flock Experiment.

Farmer Richard raised a goat kid and a lamb from birth as he would his own sons. They sat with him at the table for dinner, listened to the radio, slept on comfortable mattresses in a warm farmhouse with a solid roof over their woolly heads. When the kid became goat and lamb became sheep, the animals were put back in their respective paddocks. Despite the sudden change of environment, it was as if the goat had never been away. Within moments he was chewing on a fencepost and courting a nanny. The sheep, on the other hand, stayed away from his flock, sat himself down and was dead within a day.

Beat.

There's a lot of sheep in Chapman. We're not good with change. We flock together and don't help the lone sheep dying in the corner of the paddock. Hell, we don't even notice him.

A rumour went round town that the day Fred's dad was buried, as a harvest moon rose in the sky, Fred chopped down that tree and burnt it in his farm's only surviving paddock. For good measure, he added the dead stock that had been piling up for months. At midnight, according to the neighbouring farms, the crackling of the Finch's huge bonfire gave way to shrieking and screaming. They say that it was the remaining livestock being herded by Fred into the fire as well.

All a rumour, of course. But even so, people still ignore Fred at school. And his mum. And his sister. It's just easier to not think of them as we huddle in our comfortable mass on the other side of the paddock. Those lone sheep. That poor family. That Bonfire Boy…

SCENE TEN

Lights up on FRED *at his computer playing World Cup Soccer.*

His computer beeps that he has a message.

He is completely taken aback. He has never had a message before and doesn't quite know what to do.

His computer beeps again.

Lights up on TRAVIS *at his own computer. Although he is sending a message, we never see him type. He just speaks what he has written.*

TRAVIS: hey dude what are you doing?

FRED *clicks on the message and reads.*

FRED: 'Hey dude, what are you doing?'

He is stunned. Goes back to the game.

TRAVIS: fred mate what are you doing?

Again, FRED *checks. Smiles slightly.*

FRED: plating wrold cop succer
TRAVIS: question mark

FRED *realises his mistake.*

FRED: sorry. playing world cup soccer
TRAVIS: scored?
FRED: not yet

TRAVIS: how long you been playing?

FRED: twenty minutes into the first galf

TRAVIS: yeah?

FRED: of my fofth match

TRAVIS: god freddy youre a machine! got yourself an anorexic pop star girlfriend yet?

FRED: sorry

TRAVIS: dont apologise

FRED: sorry i meant sorry? forgot the question mark sorry

TRAVIS: youll get the hang of it mate

> *Pause.* FRED *is torn between his soccer match and* TRAVIS. *Finally he goes back to* TRAVIS.

you emailed me. thanks. was nice to hear from you

FRED: i need your help with Social Studies

TRAVIS: sure. got a great idea for an assessment.

FRED: you do? what?

TRAVIS: its called OUTBACK SOCIALISATION: ONE BOYS FIGHT TO CONQUER ISOLATION

FRED: pardon?

TRAVIS: youre a perfect case study fred. you dont have that many friends, a small family. you live on a large property in the middle of nowhere. you lost your dad to suicide…

FRED: whats that got to do with anything?

TRAVIS: thats a major rural issue fred. bring that up in a Social Studies exam, youre guaranteed extra marks.

FRED: youre talking about my dad

TRAVIS: his death was a tragic indictment on the state of rural industry. you may as well get something out of it. imagine you in thirty years time standing on your big wide verandah, your arm around your beautiful wife, your kids ploughing a lush field of wheat. imagine you overlooking your kingdom and thinking of your dad and how close you once came to losing it all.

passing this assignment is the first stepping stone to that big verandah fred.

giving your dad a legacy, despite his tragic demise

Beat.

FRED: what do i have to do?

TRAVIS: im gonna set you up with some cybermates fred. according to the latest research its important that people in isolated areas still get to have a social life. were going to test that theory

FRED: pardon?

TRAVIS: ill make sure you pass this assignment. how did you like my myspace?

FRED: was ok

TRAVIS: took me ages to put it together. what did you think of my myspace mates?

FRED: they seemed kind of weird

TRAVIS: my facebook ones are much nicer. more sophisticated

FRED: i wouldn't know

TRAVIS: well you will soon. ive told some of them about you

FRED: really?

TRAVIS: theyre our starting point fred. theyre gonna contact you and we r gonna monitor how isolated you feel. whether it makes a difference to your quality of life.

FRED: okay

TRAVIS: get you out there meeting the real people in the land of www

FRED: do you really think itll help me stay in school?

TRAVIS: if we do it right. now lets have a practice.

FRED: what?

TRAVIS: right, first lesson. you dont write 'what'. just a question mark. everythings shortened on the net

FRED: okay.

TRAVIS: nope, just 'K'.

FRED: K.

TRAVIS: K. now youre getting the hang of it!

FRED: K!

TRAVIS: now for some jargon. lol means laugh out loud. rofl means roll on the floor laughing. ttyl means talk to you later
right now chat

FRED: chat?

TRAVIS: you wanna keep these people interested you gotta be able to chat fred

FRED: how?

TRAVIS: just chat. ask me something

FRED: ummm

TRAVIS: and dont write ummm unless its for something ironic or sardonic

A long moment.

FRED: how was the party?

TRAVIS: good start fred. party was lame

Another beat.

FRED: were there girls there?

TRAVIS: lol. hardly any. the nuns changed the locks on the st catherines girls rooms. they couldn't escape. pack of penguin prison guards.
fred can I tell you something?

FRED: yes please

Beat.

TRAVIS: something happened with annette piggott. know her?

FRED: i don't know anyone

TRAVIS: shes a townie. her parents run the fish and chip shop on marine terrace

FRED: we dont go to restaurants

TRAVIS: she was down at the party skinny dipping. pissed. shouting out for her knickers. i tried to find them for her

FRED: where were they?

TRAVIS: at home on her hills hoist probably

FRED: question mark

TRAVIS: i fucked her fred. annette piggott. in the dunes. i feel terrible. have you ever cheated on someone?

FRED: not that I know of. whyd you do it?

TRAVIS: i dunno. i was drunk. not as drunk as her but drunk. she was running around with no knickers on. she threw herself at me. im so stupid

FRED: didn't anyone try to stop you?

TRAVIS: noone else knows. i made sure we did it away from the others. if any of the brothers found out id have my badge taken off me

FRED: what if annette tells someone?

TRAVIS: when I left, she was skinny dipping again, skulling passion pop and looking for the next fast food customer. she wont even remember. i hope. you wont tell anyone will you fred?

FRED: who would I tell?
TRAVIS: promise me
FRED: i promise
TRAVIS: thank you. youre a good mate

> FRED *is taken aback.*

nice chat fred! you really got the hang of it then!
FRED: thanks
TRAVIS: youre all set. remember to print out all your emails. well need them for the assignment
FRED: K.
TRAVIS: later dude
FRED: later

SCENE ELEVEN

IVY *and* FRED *sit at their kitchen table.*

IVY: Oh no…
FRED: What?
IVY: Another one's gone.
FRED: Another girl?
IVY: Might be too early to tell, they say, but it looks like it.
FRED: Who is she?
IVY: Annette Piggott. Eighteen years old. Works at her family's fish and chip shop in town.
FRED: You're kidding…

> *He takes the paper from her.*

IVY: Do you know her, love?
FRED: No. Just heard about her, that's all.
IVY: Poor thing. Her poor family. Police don't seem to know anything.
FRED: 'Last seen at a party on Whitesand Beach.' I got invited to that party.
IVY: Did you? That's exciting!
FRED: 'Police are interviewing anyone who may have seen her last…'
IVY: You should've told me—I could've organised a sitter for Becky.
FRED: 'At present, as with Elaine Thompson, Jessica Wren and Hilde Mueller, no formal leads have been established.'

IVY: Beach parties are always fun. God, the things I used to get up to in those Whitesand dunes. Would make a wharfie blush… They used to call me Poison Ivy, you know. I remember one time—

FRED: Mum, a girl has just gone missing from one of those bloody beach parties. I mean, really. What if it was Becky?

IVY: Becky's not going to any beach parties. She's twelve, for God's sake.

FRED: And how old were you when you started making wharfies blush, Poison Ivy?

Beat. IVY *won't answer.*

Thought as much.

IVY: Sorry, love. Didn't think. Poor girl.

FRED: Her name's Annette Piggott.

He keeps reading, obviously upset.

IVY: I just meant if someone's taken the time to invite you to a party, be it at the beach or in a backyard, you should go, Fred. Get out there and enjoy yourself. Boys can do that. Make the most of it, I say.

FRED: I'm fine, Mum.

IVY: I'm glad you're getting invited places. You should be getting invited places.

FRED: Leave it, Mum.

IVY: Someone's looking out for you. Is it that boy who's helping you with your Social Studies?

FRED: Yep.

IVY: How's that working out?

FRED: He's got an assessment plan for me that he reckons can't fail.

It's this internet thing. Meeting people on the internet. He thinks it'd be interesting to study how… a person in a state of isolation can find… meaningful relationships through… cyberspace… [*Beat.*] Something like that. [*He smiles shyly.*] I'm the isolated person.

IVY: Well, that sounds very scientific. Completely over my head.

FRED: It's a good idea. He's a nice guy.

She smiles. Strokes his hair as he reads the paper, concerned.

Annette Piggott…

IVY: They'll find her, Fred. Not everything ends badly. They always turn up somewhere, alive and well.

FRED: No they don't.

IVY: She'll be back at the fish and chip shop in no time.

SCENE TWELVE

FRED *at school, sitting by himself.*

Shouts, chatter, echo around him.

TRAVIS *enters. Sits nearby.*

TRAVIS: Hey.

FRED: Hey.

TRAVIS: What's wrong?

FRED: Tired. Been reading emails all night.

TRAVIS: That's great! How do you feel?

FRED: I told you—tired.

TRAVIS: I mean in a social existence kind of way.

FRED: Question mark.

TRAVIS *smiles.*

TRAVIS: You're learning fast, Freddy!

FRED: Yeah, LOL. ROFL. BTW. TTYL. Think I've got RSI.

TRAVIS: Hey, did you hear from Frida39?

FRED: Frida39... Is she the one that sees auras around budgerigars or the one that believes that Paris Hilton is Joan of Arc reincarnated?

TRAVIS: She's the one that takes photos of herself naked with garden gnomes.

FRED: Oh, Frida39. How could I forget those pictures? Yeah, I did hear from her. And Lavalips, MisterMestopholes and girlnextdoor666.

TRAVIS *laughs.*

TRAVIS: God, they work fast. What did you talk about?

FRED: Oh, you know... wormholes, emo fashion, Brangelina. Why I don't have a Myspace or a Facebook. How quaint it is that I only correspond by email. Like I'm using fucking Cobb & Co.

TRAVIS: They mean well. They're just curious, that's all. Hey, did you hear about Annette Piggott?

Beat.

FRED: Course I did. It's all over the news.

TRAVIS: Full-on, huh? Poor girl.

FRED: Poor girl? You totally took advantage of her the other night.

TRAVIS *is startled. He lowers his voice.*

TRAVIS: No I didn't. I helped her look for her knickers.

FRED: And then you had sex with her.

TRAVIS: She's eighteen, Fred! She's allowed to. If anything, she took advantage of me. I'm barely legal!

FRED: And then you left her there drunk.

TRAVIS: Fred, I got tired and came home. I tried to convince her to do the same, but she's Annette Piggott. She's got nothing else to live for but those parties. Whatever happened to her afterwards is just an unfortunate end to what I'm sure was a great night for her.

FRED: Did you prepare that?

Beat. They both look around at the other students.

Have they spoken to you? The police?

TRAVIS: Why would they need to? I wasn't the last to see her.

FRED: But you had sex with her.

TRAVIS: You're a little bit caught up on that detail, Fred. You jealous?

FRED: What? No, I don't even know her.

TRAVIS: I'm not talking about her. [*Beat.*] Look, Fred, the police aren't worried about whether Annette had sex and who it was with. This is a missing persons case. Four girls, all gone. I'm just a kid from St Isidore's. I can't help them with anything. And I don't wanna get hassled by any cops, especially with exams coming up. My stepfather would kill me. I only told you that I fucked her because I thought you were my friend. I haven't told anyone else that. Not even mysecret.com.

FRED: What's that?

TRAVIS: It's this great website where you get to tell all your secrets anonymously online. Like a confession box without the penance. It's hilarious. Frida39 got me onto it. She uses it all the time.

FRED: A woman who blogs about having sex with garden gnomes has secrets?

TRAVIS: Everyone does. Don't you? [*Beat.*] I can trust you, can't I? With what I told you?

FRED: I just feel sorry for her, that's all. I feel sorry for all of them. Those missing girls.

TRAVIS: Me too. It's scary, you know. Some weirdo right here in Chapman. [*Beat.*] So are you gonna get yourself a Myspace? A Facebook? It's more fun than email. More sociable. I can help you pick your wallpaper.

FRED: No. I don't want wallpaper. And I don't want any more of your webmates contacting me. They're not... me. I've blocked them.

TRAVIS: What? Why?

FRED: They were like a bunch of bloody blowflies, Travis. Swarming all over me, all over the screen. Telling me things about themselves I didn't want to know. Expecting me to do the same. I didn't like it. They're blocked.

TRAVIS: But what about the assignment? We haven't given it enough time to assess the isolation factor.

FRED: Travis, I've never felt more isolated in my life. If anything, all those emails made me feel more different than ever. Dumber than ever. More behind the times than ever. I don't want to do it. It's over. Tell them all to leave me alone.

TRAVIS: Everyone needs a community, Fred. We need to help each other out...

FRED: Like you did with Annette Piggott in the dunes? No thanks. Here's your iPod.

He gets it out and gives it to TRAVIS.

TRAVIS: You're blocking me too?

FRED: Yep.

TRAVIS: I was only trying to help you, Fred. Please stay in this with me. It's my job to help you.

FRED: Mother Teresa—fuck off.

TRAVIS: What about your grades?

FRED: I don't care if I get kicked out. I'm not cut out to be a farmer anyway. And I don't need you. I'm fine by myself.

TRAVIS *is stunned.*

Leave me alone, Travis. Please.

Beat.

TRAVIS: Keep the iPod. You need it more than me. My stepdad's getting me a new one anyway. If I do well in my exams.

FRED: I'm sure you will.

TRAVIS: I was only trying to help, Fred. I made a pledge.

FRED: [*with a wry laugh*] TTYL.

TRAVIS: Really?

FRED: No.

TRAVIS *leaves the iPod next to* FRED *and leaves.*

SCENE THIRTEEN

At the hospital.

TRAVIS: Case study three: Love Experiments. Through analysing couples who were in the throes of a new relationship, scientists came up with a chemical equation of sorts as to what the recipe for love is.

First of all, take some oestrogen and testosterone and mix well to form a nice batter of lust. To take the attraction a step further, add some adrenaline—be warned, this may cause a dry mouth, heart palpitations and sweating—add a drop of dopamine for ecstatic rushes of pleasure—this may cause a lack of appetite and sleeplessness—and finally mix in a dash of serotonin for constant obsessive thoughts and idealising.

For the final stage of attachment, the love recipe requires oxytocin—the chemical released during orgasm, childbirth and breastfeeding. It ensures deep bonding and an ongoing connection between partners. Add to this a big dollop of vasopressin—the chemical of devotion and protection that claims your partner as your one and only—and you should finally, finally be in love.

So that's it. That grand mystery finally solved. I don't know why we complain so much. In this age of lightning-fast wireless broadband networking and universal connection, those cyber-cupids should be working overtime. That recipe of chemicals is probably floating all around us right now, through the ether, passing through every particle of us on its way to some modem on the other side of the world. It just shouldn't be so hard, this thing called love.

SCENE FOURTEEN

FRED *sits at home doing his homework.* IVY *enters, kisses him on the head.*

IVY: Becky give you any grief?

FRED: She didn't eat her broccoli and her shower lasted seven minutes.

IVY: Seven minutes?! Little bugger. You didn't give her any dessert, did you?

> FRED *is silent.*

Freddo?

> *He looks at her.*

Freddo Frog?

FRED: Of course I gave her dessert, Mum. I'm not a total Nazi.

IVY: And I am?

FRED: Well, I didn't want to say anything, but you do appear to be growing a small moustache.

> IVY *is stunned and checks her top lip.* FRED *smiles cheekily.*

IVY: Done your homework?

FRED: It's done me.

IVY: How's your Social Studies assignment going?

FRED: Fine. Learning heaps.

IVY: Good. So what's this?

FRED: Biology.

IVY: Ooh. My specialty. Need any help?

FRED: Know anything about chromosomal mutation?

IVY: Not really. There was that lamb that had an extra leg a few years back.

FRED: Gross.

IVY: Your dad reckoned it was fantastic. Reckoned we'd make a packet if we bred them. Think of all those extra lamb shanks.

FRED: Mum…

IVY: Only problem is, breeding five-legged lambs, you'd never catch the buggers! Outrun you every time! That's what he'd say, your dad. Remember?

> *She laughs.*

FRED: No.

> *She stops laughing.*

IVY: I'll let you get on with it, then. [*Beat.*] Can I get you anything?

FRED: I'm fine, Mum.

IVY: Cup of Quik? Piece of fruit?

FRED: I'm fine.

IVY: I love you, Freddo.

FRED: Me too, Mum.

IVY: I love you.

> *She kisses him on his head. His computer beeps.* IVY *is startled.* FRED *rolls his eyes.*

What's that noise mean?

FRED: Nothing, Mum.

IVY: Not broken, is it? Bloody thing.

FRED: It's not broken, Mum. It's telling me I've got an email.

> *It beeps again.*

IVY: Persistent little bugger, isn't it?

> FRED *looks at the computer, exasperated.*

Go on then…

FRED: What?

IVY: Show me. The email thing.

FRED: Mum, you know what an email looks like. Besides, I don't wanna chat to anyone. They're all weirdos.

> *It beeps again.*

IVY: Show me.

FRED: Mum, it's not important…

IVY: It's for your assignment, isn't it? 'Course it's important. Give us a look.

> FRED *rolls his eyes and opens the email.*

IVY: Who's it from?

FRED: Probably some complete nutcase.

> IVY *reads. As she does, a girl appears across the stage. She speaks…*

IVY & SUSAN: [*together*] 'Susan Lucas.'

FRED: Susan?

IVY: Susan.

FRED: Susan what? She must have a number next to her name.

IVY: Just 'Susan Lucas'.

> FRED*'s interest is piqued.*

SUSAN: 'Hi, Fred. Hope you don't mind me contacting you. Travis sent me an email the other day and he said I should give you a poke.'

IVY: A what?

FRED: A poke, Mum. It's... cyberspeak.

IVY: Sounds awful.

SUSAN: 'My name is Susan Jane Lucas, and I go to St Mary's Catholic College in Lance Point.'

IVY: That's down south.

FRED: I know, Mum.

SUSAN: 'Travis told me some nice stuff about you. You sound really interesting. Different to anyone else online. I'd love to have you as a contact. It gets pretty lonely at this boarding school, surrounded by girls all day and all night.'

IVY: Poor thing.

SUSAN: 'Anyway, let me know what you think—I understand if you're too busy. I'm afraid I don't have a Myspace or a Facebook—I wouldn't even know how to set one of those up!'

IVY: What on earth is she talking about?

SUSAN: 'But I've attached a photo of myself if you want to put a face to the name. Hope to hear from you soon. Susan.'

    SUSAN *leaves.*

IVY: Ooh, is that her? She's a pretty little thing, isn't she?

    FRED *is stunned.*

FRED: Yeah, she is.

IVY: Are you gonna write back, Freddo?

FRED: I dunno...

IVY: You've gotta write back. She's lonely.

FRED: Mum...

IVY: Sounds lovely.

FRED: She does.

IVY: Who's this Travis boy?

FRED: Travis Masters.

IVY: Travis Masters? James Masters' boy?

FRED: Yeah.

IVY: He's the boy helping you with your Social Studies?

FRED: Yeah...

IVY: Isn't he head prefect?

FRED *nods.*

How long have you been friends?

FRED: Not long.

IVY: Good family, the Masters. Good stock.

FRED: They're not animals, Mum.

IVY: Might be. Nice breed. Hasn't got an extra leg, has he?

FRED *grins.*

Go on, love. Write back to Susan.

FRED: She'll end up being a sixty-nine-year-old vegan transsexual from Brazil.

IVY: Or she might be just who she says she is, Freddo. Look at her. She's lovely.

He looks at her photo.

FRED: She does look nice.

IVY: Go on.

She puts his hand on the mouse.

She's lovely.

He presses the mouse.

FRED: What do I say?

IVY: Tell her… 'Dear Susan. Thank you kindly for your letter…'

FRED: Email, Mum.

He types reluctantly.

IVY: 'It was really lovely to hear from you and I hope we can be friends.'

FRED: 'Lovely'?!

He keeps typing.

IVY: It's just like having a penpal again! 'Let me tell you a bit about myself…'

FRED: Oh, God…

He types.

IVY: 'I live on the outskirts of Chapman and go to school with Travis at St Isidore's Agricultural College. Our uniform is bluey green. No, wait… Teal!'

FRED: Mum, what's that got to do with anything?

IVY: She's a girl. Girls are interested in that sort of thing.

FRED: They are?

He types.

IVY: 'I am fifteen years old, have dark brown hair and I'm…'

She looks at him for a moment and then drags him to the wall and measures him.

My God, Fred! You're shooting up!

Then back to the computer.

'… and I'm five foot nine exactly.'

FRED: Mum, who cares?

IVY: Shush, Freddo, this is fun.

She pushes in and types.

'My mum calls me Freddo because when I get cross I blow my cheeks out like a frog.'

FRED *catches himself doing it and she laughs at him.*

'I like listening to music, playing computer games, and I live on a farm with my sister Becky, my mum Ivy and my da—'

She stops short. Caught out.

A long moment.

FRED: Thanks, Mum. That's a good start.

She nods.

You go have a shower. I'll keep writing to her. That's a good start.

His mother smiles.

IVY: You're shooting up, Freddo. I'm glad you're making friends. Five foot nine, hey?

She leaves. FRED *goes back to the computer, reads his email again, smiles and starts to type.*

SCENE FIFTEEN

At the police station.

SERGEANT TUKOVSKY, IVY *and* FRED *sit in the interview room.*

IVY: How you going, Freddo Frog?

FRED *says nothing.*

The doctors treat you okay?

Nothing.

Is there anything you need? Anything I can get for you?

FRED *lowers his head.*

TUKOVSKY: He's had several choc milks.

IVY: Strawberry?

TUKOVSKY: Of course. Tell me about Susan, Fred mate.

FRED *looks blankly at him.*

IVY: Fred?

He buries his head in his arms. Beat. He doesn't move.

I found all of her emails printed out in his bedroom. Sometimes she sent three a night, more on weekends. That's her. Pretty, isn't she? Susan. Look, that's her house. Her sisters. Her schnoodle.

TUKOVSKY *looks at the photos.*

TUKOVSKY: Schnoodle?

IVY: Crossbreed.

TUKOVSKY: Ugh.

IVY: He even sent off pictures of himself too, didn't you, Freddo?

Beat.

TUKOVSKY: Fred?

He sinks deeper.

IVY: I'm sorry, love. I didn't mean to be nosy. I just want to find out what's going on.

FRED *says nothing.*

TUKOVSKY: These emails, Fred? Mate, when did you last hear from Susan?

FRED: I didn't kill her. I know it looks bad, but I didn't kill her.

IVY: Fred—

TUKOVSKY: Mate, I didn't say anything about killing—

FRED: I didn't kill any of those girls. But I know who did. [*He looks directly at* TUKOVSKY.] And so should you. [*He looks down again at the blood on his hands.*] Can I wash this shit off me?

SCENE SIXTEEN

SUSAN *appears again.*

SUSAN: Hi, Fred. I'm so glad I've found someone who's actually normal on the internet. I know nothing can take the place of face-to-face conversation, but with you, even when it's all words on a computer screen, I feel like I've got a real friend. Thank you for the photos. It was beautiful seeing that you actually exist physically and not just via a dotcom title. Ever since we've been in touch, I've felt so happy. Connected. Hope that doesn't sound too corny. I love getting back to my room and checking my messages from you. I don't have many friends at school and even my contacts on the web are pretty lame, so it's so nice to have finally found a proper friend like your wonderful self. Actually, Travis emailed and told me you and he aren't speaking anymore, is that right? To be honest, I don't blame you for cutting contact. He can be a bit full of himself with all his 'good intentions'. But I guess it comes from that awful family of his. Have you met them? I haven't but I've heard about them. His mum's face doesn't move and his stepdad sold Travis' pet horse to an abattoir for dog meat. I can see why Travis tries so hard with his friends. They're all he's got. I know he adores you, Fred. I'm sure of it.

But I want to know more about you. What's your mum like? As strict as mine? Your sister sounds like a handful—you're lucky you only have one. I have two and they drive me crazy. What are your hobbies? What music do you listen to? Your favourite films? Your biggest dreams? Do you have a girlfriend? A boyfriend? Am I asking too many questions?

I hope everything is wonderful in your world, Fred. Please keep writing. It makes my day hearing from you.

Love, Susan.

Smiley face.

The sound of a printer.

Lights up on FRED. *He reads the printed email, smiles, and puts it on a growing pile.*

SCENE SEVENTEEN

Beat.

IVY: Could you give us some privacy, Barry?

TUKOVSKY: He's gotta be supervised at all times, Ive.

IVY: I'm his mum. I'll supervise.

>TUKOVSKY *doesn't move.*

I think you owe me that, Barry.

>FRED *looks at* TUKOVSKY.

TUKOVSKY: I'll be just outside the door.

>TUKOVSKY *leaves.*

IVY: Freddo.

>*He says nothing.*

Why did you do it? [*Beat.*] Everything was going so well. [*Beat.*] You told me he was your friend. [*Beat.*] What's going on, Freddo? Fred? Is it something I've done?

>FRED *pulls on his school tie.*

Don't do that, Freddo.

>*He pulls tighter.*

Freddy.

>*She tries to stop him.*

Fred!

>*She tries to release his grip but cannot. He beats her away violently.*

>*She runs to the door.*

Sergeant Tukovsky! Barry!

>TUKOVSKY *runs in and unravels the tie from* FRED's *neck.*

>FRED *screams long and loud.*

END OF ACT ONE

ACT TWO

SCENE ONE

IVY, FRED *and* TRAVIS *sit around the dinner table at Fred's house.*

TRAVIS: Thanks for the invite, Mrs Finch.

IVY: Not at all, Travis. A pleasure. An absolute pleasure. It was a bit sneaky of me, but I thought what the hell! You were surprised when you came home, weren't you, Freddo?

FRED: Yep.

TRAVIS: I can't believe you were gonna celebrate your birthday by yourself, Fred.

IVY: He's a bit of a loner, our Fred. As you know.

TRAVIS: He has let me know that, yes.

IVY: But it's his sixteenth birthday. He deserves some company. In the flesh.

TRAVIS: Well, I'm glad you thought I was the man for the job. Fred talks so much about you and Becky and the farm. It's really great to be here and see it all for myself

IVY: Does he just? All good, I hope.

TRAVIS: Absolutely.

IVY: And I can't thank you enough for helping him with his assignment, Travis. I don't quite understand the premise, but I can see it's paying off. That computer's beeping all the time with new letters.

FRED: Emails, Mum.

TRAVIS: Is it? Really. So the assignment's still working out for you, hey, Fred? Good to hear.

He looks at FRED *who is looking uncomfortable.*

It'll be good for us both to have a night off from it, Mrs Finch, after all our hard work. A nice chilled birthday just hanging out, watch some telly, just the two of us.

FRED: Telly's dead.

IVY: Becky threw a cricket ball at it last week. Bit of a tanty.

FRED: She's a bloody lunatic.

IVY: She's going through a bit of a phase, our Becky. That age. She's at a friend's place tonight. Bit of a treat for her, little shit, excuse my French, poor bugger, tough year. [*Beat.*] But it's lovely having you here. Fred hasn't had a friend over for yonks!

An awkward silence.

TRAVIS: So who's been emailing you so much, Fred, that you forgot your own birthday?

FRED: No-one.

IVY: No-one? Like hell. Susan, Travis.

TRAVIS: Susan? You and Susan Lucas are emailing each other?

IVY: Every night. Twice a night. All weekend. Quite a little friendship forming there.

TRAVIS: Are you serious?

FRED *nods.*

You didn't tell me about Susan. I thought you didn't like my webmates.

FRED: I didn't. I don't. But Susan's different. She's normal.

TRAVIS: She's a bit boring.

FRED: No, Travis. Getting naked with gnomes is boring. Sharing online astrology charts is boring. Rating YouTube videos and registering with imdb is boring.

IVY: Jesus, Fred, what language are you speaking?

FRED: Susan is not boring.

TRAVIS: She likes horseriding, Fred.

FRED: And chess.

TRAVIS: And bushwalking.

FRED: And Shakespeare.

IVY: Oh, my God, she does sound boring.

FRED *glares at his mother.*

Sorry, love.

She whispers at TRAVIS.

Hate Shakespeare. [*Aloud*] Who wants cake?

She leaves.

TRAVIS: You're a dark horse, aren't you? You told me you didn't like any of them. Told me you'd blocked them all. Told me you didn't want to take part in the assignment anymore.

FRED: I kept Susan.

TRAVIS: That's cool. I don't care. Does she talk about me?

FRED: Why?

TRAVIS: Well, I did introduce you.

FRED: She emailed me.

TRAVIS: After I told her to, Fred.

FRED: Well, we're chatting. Isn't that what you wanted?

TRAVIS: She doesn't chat with me anymore. Guess I know why now. [*Beat.*] She hasn't said anything about me? Nothing at all.

FRED: No.

Beat.

TRAVIS: Have you?

FRED: What?

TRAVIS: Mentioned me.

FRED: Not really.

TRAVIS: Why not?

FRED: We just talk about other stuff.

TRAVIS: What, I'm not important enough to either of you to mention, is that it?

FRED: No…

TRAVIS: No, I'm not important enough?

FRED: Yes…

TRAVIS: Yes, you agree I'm not important enough?

FRED: Why should you care? You've got heaps of friends. You don't need Susan.

TRAVIS: No I don't. She is boring. Each to their own, hey?

They glare at one another.

IVY *enters with cake.*

Well, this is all gonna be great material for the assignment, hey Fred?

FRED: Sure will, Trav.

IVY *beams.*

IVY: So what are you boys gonna get up to tonight?

FRED: Whatever it is that isolated rural youth do, I guess. Take drugs. Get pissed. Roll around in the dunes.

Beat.

TRAVIS: Why don't we check out the missing girls' Facebooks?

IVY: What's that?

TRAVIS: It's like your own personal online life, Mrs Finch. Where you can say what you want. Be who you want. Play the role you've always wanted to play. All the girls are on there, even Annette Piggott. They can't shut them down because as far as they know, they're still alive. It's like the cops are waiting for them to log on. To leave some hint as to where they are, what they're doing.

FRED: That's really creepy, Travis.

TRAVIS: No, it's not. It's beautiful. Even if they're dead, their loved ones can still talk to them. They can even leave messages for them. From one ether to another. Annette's parents left a message saying that they love her and they miss her but that they'll have to replace her at the fish and chip shop. Since she went missing, business has gone through the roof, but they're down a worker.

IVY: That's awful.

TRAVIS: And Elaine's sister writes on hers every day. She's only eight and she keeps asking what heaven is like and why God won't let Elaine update her status. So cute.

IVY: You can talk to the dead?

FRED: No, Mum. No-one can do that.

TRAVIS: Come on—let's log on and leave a message.

FRED: I can't do that. I didn't know any of them.

TRAVIS: It's cyberspace, Fred. Who really knows anyone?

FRED: Me and Susan do.

TRAVIS: Sorry—except you and Susan. Come on—log on.

FRED: I don't feel right about it. Let's just email Susan. At least we both know her.

TRAVIS: I used to know her. No great loss. There's only so much italic purple writing and smiley faces a man can take. She's all yours. [*He smiles charmingly at* IVY.] That was a lovely dinner, Mrs Finch.

IVY: Call me Ivy, Travis.

TRAVIS: Ivy. It's so great to have a good home-cooked meal. The boarding house can be a little Dickensian sometimes.

> IVY *stares at him blankly.*

The food's mush. It feels good getting my teeth into some meat for a change, you know? Those lamb shanks were delicious.

He tucks into his cake. IVY *is charmed.*

IVY: You know, Travis, we had a five-legged lamb /once.

FRED: /Mum /

IVY: /Shush, Freddo—my husband Jim said we should /breed them…

FRED: /Mum, /please…

IVY: /Think of all the extra chops we could sell, he'd say.

> FRED *groans.*

Only problem would/ be…

FRED: /Mum! /

IVY & TRAVIS: [*together*] How would you ever catch them?!

> *Beat, then* IVY *and* TRAVIS *laugh.* FRED *watches on, stunned.*

IVY: Well, I'd best be off. Shelves don't stack themselves, unfortunately.

> FRED *is mortified.*

> TRAVIS *stands.*

TRAVIS: It was wonderful meeting you at last, Ivy. Sorry if I was a bit rude over dinner. Susan's a pretty lady. Got a bit jealous. Sorry, Freddo.

> FRED *says nothing.*

IVY: Fred. Travis just apologised to you.

> *Still nothing.*

Fred!

FRED: No worries, Travis. I'm sorry too.

TRAVIS: You sure you're right to get to work, Ivy? I've got my L-plates—I could drive you. It's not too safe in town right now for ladies.

IVY: Thank you, Travis, but I'm fine. I think I'm a bit old for whoever's taking those girls. He seems to like them young.

TRAVIS: Don't sell yourself short, Ivy. You're in your prime.

FRED: Like a piece of rump steak.

IVY: Lovely having you over, Travis. Toodle-oo.

FRED: Toodle-oo? What are you, eighty?

IVY: Christ. I've never used that word in my life. I'm only thirty-five, Travis.

TRAVIS: Toodle-oo, Ivy. See you soon, I hope.

IVY: 'Bye, Freddo Frog. Love you.

FRED: 'Bye, Mum.

IVY: Love you!

FRED: Yep.

Beat.

TRAVIS: He says he loves you too, Ivy.

She leaves, smiling.

FRED: She doesn't know I've quit the assignment. I didn't realise she'd called you. You may as well go home.

TRAVIS: No, I'll stay. She meant well. She's awesome. Beats my mum any day. The last joke my mum told was out of a Christmas cracker three years ago, and even then she had to have it explained to her. Xanax will do that to you. You're lucky to have such a cool mum. One that's around all the time, you know. I feel like when my dad died I lost my mum too.

He leaves the table. Looks around.

FRED: What was it? The joke in the Christmas cracker?

TRAVIS: Is that where it happened?

He is looking out the window. Beat.

FRED: Yeah.

TRAVIS: Jim Finch. Loving husband and father. Well-respected local identity. Member of the Chapman football team, the Lions Club. Adored his family.

FRED: That was his death notice.

TRAVIS: I know. *Chapman Gazette* online.

FRED: Why'd you look that up?

TRAVIS: Why did he do it like that? Surely he knew it'd be one of his own family that'd find him. Surely he could've chosen a better way than that.

FRED: A better way?

TRAVIS: He could've driven into a tree on the highway, gassed himself in a carpark, walked into the ocean. But he chose to do it right here, in full sight of his family. You must be pretty angry about that.

Your last memory of him should've been playing football or ploughing or sharing a beer with him on the verandah. Not purple and lifeless and hanging from a branch next to Becky's swing.

FRED: How did you know about the swing?

TRAVIS: Google.

FRED: You're kidding…

> TRAVIS *smiles.*

TRAVIS: Zac Taylor's dad was one of the ambulance officers that day. Word gets around in Chapman, Fred. People know stuff about people. Who's getting the sack, who's pregnant, who's fucking whose wife.

> FRED *is startled. Looks at* TRAVIS, *shocked.*

I understand you wanting some time alone.
Must've been awful. Finding him there like that. I know how that feels, Freddo. You never forget what they look like at that last moment. It's not the way you want to remember them.

> *A long beat.*

FRED: A month before Dad… I wagged school. Spent the day down the creek, yabbying. I heard Dad leave and then not long after another car pulled in. It was Barry Tukovsky—that policeman. He'd never been out here before, as far as I could remember. I only knew him because of the drug talks he gave at school sometimes. But he seemed to know his way round our house like he'd been here heaps of times. Like he was one of us. I watched him from across the paddock. He went round the back, took off his boots—just like Dad—and went inside. Then I got worried. I thought something must've happened. I thought Becky might be in trouble, so I ran down to see what was going on. But when I got here they were…

I watched the whole thing. It was kind of nice, in a way. He made Mum smile. Laugh. He touched her so gently. I hadn't seen Dad touch Mum in ages, not even when she passed him the salt.

It was nice to watch. It was. But it didn't stop me from putting a huntsman in Tukovsky's boot before he left.

I wagged school every Thursday for a month after that. Watched them every time, quietly, through the keyhole, right up until the day…

> *He catches himself. A beat.* TRAVIS *is still close.*

I was here, Travis. That day. While Mum and Sergeant Tukovsky were fucking I was watching them. While I was watching them, Dad was hanging himself right there in the backyard. All of us so caught up in our own worlds we didn't even notice. Not for hours.

That Thursday.

Mum reckons he did it for the life insurance. She doesn't know I know.

TRAVIS: I reckon your dad knew too, Fred. I hope he didn't, but I reckon he did.

> FRED *is stunned.* TRAVIS *touches him gently.*

But I won't tell anyone, Fred. I promise. That sort of a story could turn a town against you. Your family's already been through enough. I'll look after you. I promise.

FRED: Travis… you really don't know anything about Annette Piggott going missing?

TRAVIS: If you want me to, I can go to the cops and let them know I saw her that night. I'd do that for you, if it'd make you feel better.

FRED: Nah. Don't trust the cops in this town anyway.

TRAVIS: Don't blame you, mate. Don't blame you.

> *Beat.*

FRED: Want some more cordial?

TRAVIS: Sure. Mix it with this. [*He gets out a bottle of vodka and pours some into the cordial cups.*] To isolated friendship.

FRED: To isolated friendship.

> *They clink cups and drink.*

> TRAVIS *smiles at* FRED.

> *Beat.*

> *He leans in to* FRED *and strokes his hair.* FRED *is frozen.*

> *He touches* FRED*'s face softly. His fingers run over his eyes, his cheek, his mouth.*

> FRED *still doesn't move.*

> TRAVIS *moves in to kiss him.*

No.

TRAVIS: Freddo—

FRED: No. I love Susan.

TRAVIS: Susan—

FRED: No. Go.

TRAVIS: Freddo, I was just trying to—

FRED: Go.

> TRAVIS *gathers his things.*

TRAVIS: I'm sorry.

> *As* TRAVIS *leaves,* FRED *goes to his computer and turns it on.*

SCENE TWO

The police station.

FRED *is asleep in the corner, curled up tightly in a ball.*
IVY *and* SERGEANT TUKOVSKY *sit together.*

IVY: Five foot nine, he is now. Don't let it fool you. He's still a little boy.
TUKOVSKY: You right, Ive?

> *He goes to hold her hand.*
>
> *She whispers...*

IVY: Don't you bloody dare.
TUKOVSKY: I'm sorry. Just trying to help.
IVY: Help? With what, Barry?
TUKOVSKY: I know it's a difficult time.
IVY: Really? You've learnt to spot that now, have you?
TUKOVSKY: Ive,,,
IVY: Where have you been? Where did you go?
TUKOVSKY: I'm sorry, Ivy.
IVY: Eighteen months and not a bloody peep from you, you bastard. How could you do that to me?

> *Beat.*

You should've seen me trying to fill them all in on what I was doing at the 'approximate time of death', Barry. They didn't notice my pretty dress. Or that I had make-up and perfume on. Or that I'd stripped the bedsheets off. Bloody country cops. No eye for detail.

They just wanted to know what I hadn't noticed. Like my husband tying a rope to the eucalypt outside. Swinging there through the window. You could see that tree easily from the bedroom, you know.
TUKOVSKY: I know. Now.
IVY: We should've seen him, Barry. We should've found him. Not Fred. He'd been hanging there all afternoon.

TUKOVSKY: I stayed as long as I could, Ivy.

IVY: Bullshit, Barry. You took off like a bloody brumby.

TUKOVSKY: What else could I do? Your husband killed himself and I was first on the scene because I was having a fling with his wife. I'd only just left your bed when I got the call and had to head back to cut him down. I thought he was in town. It was Thursday.

IVY: Every Thursday like bloody clockwork. Just a 'fling', was I?

TUKOVSKY: No, Ive… of course not. I'm sorry I didn't stick around. But I did notice your lipstick and your smell. All over me. So I cut him down and then I got the hell out of there.

IVY: You left me to deal with their questions.

TUKOVSKY: Ivy, this is a small town. Any whiff of a scandal and your name's mud. I didn't want that to happen to you so I removed myself from the investigation.

IVY: How noble of you, Barry. Told your wife that yet? I see her all the time down the IGA, you know. She asked me once where the sauce aisle was.

> *Beat.*

TUKOVSKY: Do you think he knew?

IVY: He didn't know. We were too careful.

TUKOVSKY: But he killed himself, Ivy.

IVY: We were going broke, Barry. He did it for the insurance. He did it to keep the farm in the family and to put Fred through that bloody ag school. There's no water, the crops failed, the stock died and then so did the farmer.

TUKOVSKY: What if he knew? What if he saw me one Thursday, parked in the back paddock, waiting for him to go? A farmer knows what goes on on his property.

IVY: You think it's never crossed my mind, Barry? Me with my legs up round your ears while my husband hangs himself through the window? I don't know what's worse some days—knowing that we may have been doing that while he was still alive or that we were doing it while he was swinging there dead. Either way, his eyes still open. Looking straight at the house.

> *Beat.*

But he didn't know. I checked. After all those coppers left I went up to that tree and sat on that branch and looked at the bedroom window and he wouldn't have seen a thing. That bloody sun may have killed him but it also saved him from seeing anything while he died. So there you go, Barry. Absolved.

TUKOVSKY *looks relieved.*

But I couldn't care less about either of you now, Sergeant. Both as gutless as each other. Both left me to deal with it all.

I just want to see my little boy right. He's a good boy and he's been through enough.

You make sure you get to the bottom of this, Barry. You owe me that.

SCENE THREE

TRAVIS *in the hospital.*

TRAVIS: Case study four: The Strip Search Prank Caller. More of a scam than an experiment.

In the US, a prank caller posing as a police officer called popular fast food outlets to encourage the managers to strip their workers and sexually abuse them. Over fifty-five per cent of the fast food bosses went through with the abuse, believing that if the police encouraged it, then it was okay. The hoaxer made the calls for a period of ten years before being arrested. He was found not guilty, of course. After all, he wasn't responsible. He wasn't at any of the scenes. He'd left no DNA. All he'd done was pick up the phone and make a suggestion—one human being to another.

SCENE FOUR

FRED *is on his computer. It beeps that a message has come through.*
SUSAN *enters across the stage.*

SUSAN: freddy are you there?
FRED: hi susan. yep
SUSAN: how is everything?
FRED: good
SUSAN: did you have a good birthday?
FRED: not really. mum cooked dinner. travis came around

SUSAN: how is travis?

FRED: why do you ask?

SUSAN: i got a weird email from him. he seemed kind of angry

FRED: what does it say?

SUSAN: wait a sec. ill forward it to you

He waits. A beep. He reads it.

FRED: jesus. are you ok?

SUSAN: just gave me a bit of a scare thats all. ive never heard him talk like that

FRED: maybe we should go to the cops

SUSAN: no. hes just jealous. im more worried about you. hes pretty angry. what happened exactly?

Beat.

FRED: he tried to kiss me

SUSAN: question mark, exclamation mark

FRED: he tried to kiss me. i think he has a crush on me

SUSAN: no way. travis is every girls dream. theres no way. he was probably just mucking around

FRED: don't think so. didn't seem like it

SUSAN: what did you do?

FRED: told him to fuck off

SUSAN: you didn't say that. i hope

FRED: i did. i hate him

SUSAN: question mark

FRED: i do. i hate him

A long beat.

susan?

SUSAN: he cant help it if he feels that way about you. you should be kinder. no wonder hes angry. hes embarrassed

FRED: i didn't want to kiss him

SUSAN: you should probably stay away from him fred. hes obviously struggling with something. make sure you stay safe

FRED: now youre freaking me out

SUSAN: that email was a bit weird. plus, have you ever heard the rumours about how his dad died?

FRED: i thought he fell out of a tractor
SUSAN: just be careful. sounds like hes pretty angry right now
FRED: from the sounds of that email hes ready to kill me
SUSAN: or me

> *A long pause. They sit, frightened.*

> you know the best way to kill someone?
FRED: how?
SUSAN: a knife. lower left side of the abdomen. guaranteed death
FRED: how do you know that?
SUSAN: i read it online somewhere
FRED: why would you tell me that?
SUSAN: you read the email. i just want you to be safe
FRED: i reckon hes bluffing
SUSAN: i hope so. sorry. it just gave me a scare
FRED: youll be ok.
SUSAN: are you sure you weren't giving out any signals fred?
FRED: no way. im not gay
SUSAN: are you sure? how do you know?
FRED: i just know
SUSAN: but how?

> *A long moment. Finally* FRED *speaks.*

FRED: because I lobe you
SUSAN: you lobe me? is that some new cyberjargon ive never heard of?

> *A long beat.* FRED *looks mortified.* SUSAN *waits.*

FRED: no. just a typo

> SUSAN *smiles.*

SUSAN: i lobe you too fred
FRED: question mark
SUSAN: i lobe you too
FRED: what? why?
SUSAN: because youre you
FRED: how long have you lobed me?
SUSAN: awhile. since around your third email
FRED: why didn't you say anything?
SUSAN: why didn't you?

A long beat.

this is weird

FRED: i know. i don't know what to write

Another long beat.

SUSAN: are you a virgin?

FRED: yes

SUSAN: me too

TRAVIS *enters and sits next to* SUSAN.

FRED: really? i thought i was the only one

SUSAN/TRAVIS: ive never even kissed anyone

FRED: me neither

SUSAN/TRAVIS: maybe you could be my first

FRED: really? how?

SUSAN/TRAVIS: im going to come to chapman

TRAVIS: i reckon we should meet somewhere really nice, like on those old movies, and spot each other from afar and without saying a word, ill just know youre fred and youll know im susan and well sit and talk face to face until the sun sets. or is that totally bizarre?

FRED: no that sounds awesome

TRAVIS: and then we can kiss. and touch. and hold hands. and smell each others breath

FRED: ill take you to the dunes

TRAVIS: what happens in the dunes?

FRED: whatever we want. will you really come?

TRAVIS: ill really come

FRED: when?

TRAVIS: give me two weeks. ill sort it out

FRED: i cant believe this

TRAVIS: believe it. i lobe you fred

FRED: i lobe you susan

TRAVIS: and fred—I mean it. watch out for travis. stay safe. if we get any more weird emails well tell the police. they'll look out for us. but in the meantime, stay safe. smiley face

FRED: smiley face

SCENE FIVE

IVY *reads a magazine at the table, singing a Beyonce song as she reads.*
FRED *enters, his hair combed, a little nervous.* IVY *looks up and is momentarily taken aback.*

IVY: Freddo Frog.
FRED: What?
IVY: What do you mean 'what'? Look at you! You look just like… [*Beat.*] You look so handsome.

    FRED *looks pleased.*

FRED: Can you do this up for me?

    He goes to her. She ties his tie.

IVY: What's all this in aid of? Who are you trying to impress?

    He grins.

FRED: She's here, Mum. Susan. She's come up to Chapman for the weekend and asked if we could meet. Do I look okay?
IVY: Susan's here?
FRED: Do I look okay?
IVY: You look gorgeous. She's in Chapman?
FRED: Yep.
IVY: Gorgeous.

    Beat. They stare at one another.

FRED: Mum… this is my first… you know…
IVY: First what?
FRED: My first… date.
IVY: Oh, darling. Where you going?
FRED: Rotary Park. By the lake.

    IVY *smiles.*

IVY: The lake… [*Beat. Her smile fades.*] Bit smelly there, right now, Freddo. Near dry and full of rotting algae.
FRED: Oh, bum… Bum, bum, bum…
IVY: But it's blowing an easterly. You should be right.

    She smoothes his hair. Beat.

FRED: I really like her, Mum.
IVY: I can see that.
FRED: She's lovely.
IVY: I know.
FRED: She's come all this way to see me.
IVY: She must like you.
FRED: She's lovely. Really lovely.
IVY: So you've said.

> *She smiles at him. Beat.*

FRED: Mum… could you do something for me?
IVY: I know what you're gonna ask, Fred.
FRED: Is it that obvious?
IVY: You're a teenager. That's what teenagers do.
FRED: Do you mind?
IVY: Of course not. You take her softly—by her hand is nice, or holding the shoulders nice and gentle, like this…

> FRED *looks confused.*

… and then you lean in slowly—make eye contact most of the way…
FRED: Mum…
IVY: Shush. And then, just like on the movies, when you're close enough to feel each other's breath, close your eyes and drink each other in through the kiss.
FRED: Mum…
IVY: Your lips should be just a little bit moist—not too much—and it's nice to keep it soft the first time. Soft and sweet…

> *She opens her eyes, just inches from his face.* FRED *is staring at her in horror. Beat.*

What?
FRED: I only wanted a lift into town.
IVY: Oh. I thought you wanted to know how to—
FRED: No! God, what is with everyone in this place?
IVY: Sorry, love. Sorry.
FRED: No, no, no!
IVY: I wasn't gonna go all the way!
FRED: Mum, shut up!

Beat. She smiles.

IVY: You found your dad's aftershave.

She straightens his tie.

Lost myself for a moment. You bugger. Lost myself.

FRED: Were you really thinking of Dad then?

IVY: What a question, Fred!

FRED: Were you?

IVY: Of course I was. [*Beat.*] Come on then, Romeo. I'll drive you in.

SCENE SIX

TRAVIS *in the hospital.*

TRAVIS: Case study five.

Professor Harry Harlow experimented with how love developed between mother and child. He got a group of baby macaque monkeys—the animal most similar to your average human child— separated them into two cages and placed a surrogate mother into each. One mother was made from wire. The other was made from terry towelling and warmed from within by a light bulb. Both of the mothers were also given a rubber breast from which the monkeys could feed.

The monkeys in the wire mother's cage showed no interest in the breast. They stayed away from her, grew weak and became more and more isolated. The monkeys in the terry towelling mother's cage, however, suckled and cuddled and clung tight to their surrogate mum and only ever got upset when Harlow removed her from their cage.

Going a step further, Harlow then removed the breast of the terry towelling mother.

The monkeys still flocked to her and embraced her tighter than ever before, even after she'd been removed for long periods and then returned. Those little babies couldn't get enough of that warmth, that maternal glow.

Later, Harlow created a new surrogate mother called 'The Iron Maiden'. Again, the mother was made of soft terry towelling, but this time, without warning, she would stab her babies with a metal spike or blow gusts of freezing cold air on them. Despite this cruelty, the babies would always return to her and compete for her affection. The conclusion is that comfort is far more important than feeding, and that so long as there is a beating heart to place his ear against in times of need, a child will willingly face hunger and pain. Even if the one he loves most stabs him deep, bleeds him dry, the little monkey will keep demanding love, will risk his own safety, will always come back for more of that warm, soft, mother's embrace.

SCENE SEVEN

IVY *is leaving the IGA supermarket. As she fumbles for her keys she looks around nervously.*

Suddenly...

TRAVIS: Ivy.

> *She leaps. Drops her bag.*

IVY: Jesus! Oh, Travis. Jesus, you scared the life out of me.
TRAVIS: Sorry. Let me get that for you.

> *He kneels at her feet and repacks her handbag.*

IVY: What are you doing here? No parties on tonight?
TRAVIS: There is. Didn't wanna go. Drink?

> *He gets out a hipflask.*

IVY: God, this takes me back. What is it?
TRAVIS: It's a good Tasmanian pinot actually. Only the best.

> *She laughs and takes a swig.*

IVY: Mmm. A nice soft palate with undertones of Beam and Coke.

> *She takes a bigger swig.*

TRAVIS: How's Fred?
IVY: Great. He's on his date with Susan.

> *Beat.*

TRAVIS: Is he? Where?
IVY: Rotary Park. So cute. It's nice of you to leave them alone for the night. You're a good mate, aren't you?

TRAVIS: I do what I can.

He drinks.

IVY: It was so exciting tonight, Travis. He was all flushed and gorgeous. Your project has really brought the best out in him. You could probably give him some tips, though. When it comes to girls, I'm afraid Fred's a bit of a novice.

He hands her back the hipflask. She has another drink.

I know what those other boys call him. What people say. You're a good mate.

TRAVIS: I love him. [*Beat.*] I really do. I'm not an expert on parents, Ivy. I'm not around mine enough to know exactly what kind of a job they do, exactly what they offer the world as people. But I can tell what other people's parents are like. And I reckon Fred's got the cream of the crop.

IVY: I think Becky might dispute you on that one. Little bugger smacked me one the other day. Can't blame her. Been a tough year.

TRAVIS: You can see how much Fred loves you.

IVY: Really?

TRAVIS: Yeah. When he talks about you his eyes look different. They take on this new light. Soft but strong. Protective.

IVY: He has his dad's eyes.

TRAVIS: He has your smile.

IVY: He's a good boy. I was worried about him for awhile there. What he did with that bonfire…

TRAVIS: So he really did kill those animals? Herded them into the fire?

IVY: Have you ever tried herding live animals into a fire? It's impossible. Call yourself a farmer… [*Beat.*] He slaughtered them all first. Slit their throats. Then he set them on fire. You lot should get your facts straight.

TRAVIS: We all do stupid things when we're upset. Emotions just get the better of us sometimes. We're only human. I'll make sure no-one ever calls him Bonfire Boy again.

IVY: He's lucky to have you as a friend.

TRAVIS: He's lucky to have such a great mum.

They smile at one another.

IVY: What about you? No girls to see tonight? Or are they all too scared to come out?

TRAVIS: I'm not interested in them anyway, boys or girls. It's always the same. A bunch of bored kids running around with fake ids and cheap beer. Pocketfuls of pills and banana-flavoured condoms. Little boys desperate to lose their virginity and little girls desperate to assist them. It's boring. I've grown out of all that.

IVY: Have you?

TRAVIS: Yeah, been there, done that. I'm looking for something a little more satisfying now. A little more mature. Strong, funny… sexy. Like you. [*Beat.*] Sorry. That was rude of me.

IVY: No, it wasn't. It wasn't.

TRAVIS: It was disrespectful.

IVY: I'm only thirty-five, Travis. I'm quite happy to be called sexy. Been a while since anyone's said it. God, the air is freezing tonight.

She drinks.

TRAVIS: There should be more people like you in this town, Ivy. It'd make the place a lot more interesting.

IVY: Yeah, I could do wonders for Chapman tourism. 'Come see Ivy Finch, Chapman widow. Marvel at her empty farm! Laugh out loud at her foil highlights! Gasp in awe at her oddball kids and take in the amazing spectacle of her sexy IGA uniform.'

She laughs and rifles through her bag for her keys.

TRAVIS: Don't make fun of yourself. I think you're beautiful.

He takes her bag and puts it down on the ground. He travels up her body slowly then reaches her face.

You are absolutely divine.

He reaches out to touch her.

You must miss it, Ivy. Being touched. Wrapping yourself around someone. Feeling their breath on your face. Having a man speak to you in a secret language only the two of you know.

IVY: What are you playing at, Travis?

TRAVIS: I love it when you say my name.

Beat.

IVY: Travis…

TRAVIS: I've been waiting here all night for you, Ivy. I can't stop thinking about you. I want to be close to you. Curl up inside your belly under your skin and stay there. Warm and safe and sexy.

IVY: Travis, you're only sixteen…

TRAVIS: And you're only thirty-five. You're in your prime, Ivy.

IVY: [*laughing nervously*] Like a good piece of rump.

TRAVIS: I want to take you down the Whitesand dunes. Away from that farm. I want to unzip this silly dress and look at you. See you naked in the moonlight, lying on the sand. You remember what that feels like, don't you, Ivy? Cool and soft under your back. Holding the sand tight in your hands. I want to take you there, Ivy. And I want to kiss you here…

He touches her eyes softly…

And here…

He touches her cheek…

And here…

He touches her mouth.

I want to taste you. Every part of you. I think you'd be delicious. Salty like the ocean, sweaty like the earth. Let me taste you. Let me take you down the dunes like when you were a girl, Ivy, and taste you

IVY: I can't do that.

TRAVIS: You can.

IVY: I shouldn't.

TRAVIS: Please. Come on. Let's go.

IVY: Fred will be home soon. He might need me.

TRAVIS: I need you more.

IVY: Becky…

TRAVIS: Is at Mrs Haigh's house till the morning.

IVY: Travis…

TRAVIS: You said it again. I'm going to take you to the dunes. Right now. You deserve it.

IVY: We shouldn't go to the dunes. It's not safe there. The girls.

TRAVIS: You're not a girl, Poison Ivy. Besides, I'll look after you.

IVY: Poison Ivy. That's what they used to call me…

TRAVIS: Show me why.

SCENE EIGHT

The police interview room.

FRED *and* IVY *and* TUKOVSKY.

SERGEANT TUKOVSKY: What happened to Susan, Fred?

> FRED *lowers his head. Devastated.*

> Fred. It's getting late. If you know anything about those missing girls, I'm the man you should tell.

FRED: Why? You're not in charge anymore.

TUKOVSKY: I'm in constant contact with the city detectives. I'm more than capable of passing this information onto them. Don't you question my authority.

FRED: Don't talk to me like you're my dad.

IVY: Fred. Enough.

TUKOVSKY: You better start bloody talking, mate. The cops in the city won't treat you this well.

IVY: Go easy, Barry. He's just a little boy.

TUKOVSKY: Little boy, my arse. He's just gutted someone, Ivy. Disembowelled him on the street. You wanna talk about little boys, you should spare a thought for Travis Masters alone in his hospital bed. This one put him there. And now he's going on about the missing girls. So no more bullshit, Fred. Time to answer some questions.

> FRED *raises his head.*

FRED: K.

TUKOVSKY: Good. First things first. Why'd you stab Travis Masters?

> FRED *reaches into his shoe. He gets out some folded paper. Unfolds it. Smoothes it.*

FRED: I waited for her. Susan. I waited for her all night on that bench by that stinking lake. She never showed up. I thought that maybe she'd been held up. Or she'd missed the bus. Or maybe she'd heard about Bonfire Boy and had decided she didn't love me at all. I walked home. When I got there, this was stuck to my bedroom window.

> *He places the paper in front of* TUKOVSKY. TUKOVSKY *reads it.*

TUKOVSKY: mysecret.com 77493, 77862, 99114, 106426.

FRED: It's a website. You might want to have a look.

TUKOVSKY *opens his laptop. Beat.*

TUKOVSKY: Uh… could you…?

FRED *takes over.*

It's a new program. Haven't quite got it sussed yet.

FRED *brings up the webpage.*

FRED: I went home and looked at the secrets under those numbers. This is 77493.

TUKOVSKY: 'Today I had a whore named ET. Was over quickly. Money well spent though.' ET?

FRED: Now look at this one. A week later. 77862.

TUKOVSKY: 'Today I made a barmaid cry. She smelt like stale beer but I actually quite liked her.'

FRED: Are you starting to get it now? 99114.

TUKOVSKY: 'Picked up a Swedish girl down by the beach. Left her there as well. She kept giggling and I got really angry. She won't be getting home in a hurry.'

FRED: Hilde Mueller. Now this one. Read this one.

TUKOVSKY: '106426. Had fish and chips in the dunes today. Threw them away. They tasted disgusting.'

IVY: The dunes?

FRED: 201009.

TUKOVSKY: 'Tonight I'm going to fuck my best friend's girlfriend. Fuck her right up, just like all the others.' Christ in a sidecar.

FRED: I looked at the history of that particular secret-keeper. He only has one other entry. 23774.

TUKOVSKY: 'My dad didn't fall out of the tractor that day. I pushed him.' I don't understand that one. [*To* IVY] Do you?

IVY *shakes her head.*

FRED: All of the dates correspond to the missing girls. Elaine Thompson right through to Annette Piggott—all of them. I'm the best friend and Susan is my girlfriend. Check!

TUKOVSKY: This is insane. There's no way this could happen…

FRED: There was one more thing stuck to my window. This.

He gets out another printout. TUKOVSKY *recoils.*

TUKOVSKY: Jesus Christ!

IVY: What does it say? What is it? Barry?

TUKOVSKY: It's a photo, Ivy.

> TUKOVSKY *passes it to* IVY. *She looks at it, horrified.*

IVY: Oh, my God.

TUKOVSKY: Interview terminated.

> *He switches off the tape recorder.*

IVY: Barry, I…

TUKOVSKY: This is too much.

IVY: Freddo…

TUKOVSKY: I'm gonna have to hand this over, Ivy.

IVY: No, Barry. Please.

TUKOVSKY: The city detectives will know better than me.

IVY: Please don't get them involved.

TUKOVSKY: What the hell were you thinking, Ivy?

> TUKOVSKY *leaves the interview room.*
>
> *A long moment.* IVY *is transfixed by the photo.*

FRED: Why'd you do that, Mum?

IVY: Freddo, I'm so sorry. I didn't know he had a camera.

FRED: He was gonna come after you, Mum. He was gonna kill you. Then Becky maybe. Who knows when he'd stop? That's why I did what I did. You would've been his next secret.

> *A long moment. Then* IVY *looks around. Starts gathering her things. She pokes her head out the door.*

IVY: Come on. We're going.

FRED: What? Where?

IVY: We're going to the hospital. We're going to get that little bastard.

FRED: Mum, we can't—

IVY: I'm not letting some little flaccid runt destroy my son's life. You've done nothing wrong, Fred. Come on. We're going.

FRED: Mum, I'm in custody.

IVY: Well, I'm your mother. Now move, Fred.

FRED: Mum—

IVY: *Now!*

FRED *gets up.* IVY *checks one more time and they leave the interview room.*

SCENE NINE

TRAVIS *in the hospital.*

TRAVIS: Case study six. In the sixteenth century, Dr Thomas Muffet was keen to impress Queen Elizabeth the First with his vast medical knowledge. He had heard the virgin Queen was terrified of spiders and so made it his mission to test every species in England in order to determine which was the most venomous and then come up with some way to eradicate them and thus satisfy the arachnophobic queen. Unfortunately, he could find no-one willing to be bitten by the hundreds of spiders he gathered for his test, and so instead he sat down his little daughter Patience and used her as his subject. Each day he sat her down with some curds and whey—her favourite dessert—and let the spiders do their worst. He wasn't worried about her having a fatal reaction. She was, after all, just a weak little child. She was expendable. And so the experiment continued.

Thankfully, England has never had any venomous spiders, so Patience survived, but never trusted her father again and ran away not long after the experiment ended. Elizabeth the First showed no interest in Dr Muffet's crazy experiment—she probably knew exactly how Patience felt, being tortured and sacrificed for her father. Heartbroken, Dr Muffet told his story to a friend named Elizabeth Goose who turned the whole thing into a five-line poem. A dark, insane, potentially fatal experiment is now a nursery rhyme that can be quoted by any child you meet in the street. Everything that is dark has a heart of innocence. I'm sure Dr Muffet meant well. All he wanted was his queen.

FRED *and* IVY *enter the hospital room.*

The three look at each other for a long moment.

Then...

Are you okay, Fred?

FRED *is taken aback. He nods.*

Ivy?

IVY *glares at* TRAVIS.

I'm gonna pull through. You got me in a good spot, Fred. They reckon if there's one place to be stabbed, that's where you got me.

FRED: That's not what I heard.

TRAVIS: You should've googled it. More reliable than hearsay.

FRED: If I could do it again I'd slit your throat.

IVY: Fred. Shush now.

TRAVIS: Did you bail him out, Ivy? That must've cost a bit.

FRED: What did you do to Susan?

TRAVIS: I don't know what you're talking about.

FRED: Why couldn't you just let me have what I wanted? Why couldn't you just leave us alone?

TRAVIS: If it wasn't for me you wouldn't have even met Susan.

IVY: He never got to meet her, you little prick.

TRAVIS: It's not all bad. You met me. I met you.

IVY: You're sick.

TRAVIS: I'm sick?! You completely took advantage of me. I'm barely legal.

IVY: What have you done with those girls?

TRAVIS: You should have seen her, Fred. She couldn't get enough. It was like being thrown to the lions.

FRED: Don't talk about my mum like that. Tell me what you did to Susan. Where have you left her?

TRAVIS: Why? Are people looking?

IVY: The city cops are onto you, Travis. You and your dirty little secrets.

TRAVIS: You're one to talk, Ivy.

SERGEANT TUKOVSKY *barges in.*

TUKOVSKY: Ivy, you're in a shitload of trouble for this.

TRAVIS: I couldn't have put it better myself. What have you got to ask me, Sergeant?

TUKOVSKY *looks confused. He looks to* IVY.

FRED: Ask him? Arrest him. He killed Susan.

IVY: Let the sergeant do his job, Fred.

FRED: And the other girls.

TUKOVSKY: Fred!

FRED: We found your secrets, Travis. We read what you wrote on that website. We know what you did to all of them, those girls. [*To* TUKOVSKY] He fucked Annette in the sand dunes the night she went missing. Then Susan. Then—

TRAVIS *looks at* IVY. *She looks away.*

TRAVIS: Hang on. Before we start… [*He gets out his phone.*] Best we keep it official, hey, Sergeant? So that there's absolutely no doubt as to what gets said in here. New phone. Does everything. Even records voice.

TUKOVSKY: If you want this to be official you should have a lawyer present, Travis. I'm just here to take these two back to the station. The city cops will be dealing with you. They're on their way.

TRAVIS *starts recording.*

TRAVIS: I don't need a lawyer. I haven't done anything wrong.

FRED: Bullshit.

TRAVIS: Either way, I'd rather record it. It's for the assignment, you know.

FRED: What?

TRAVIS: The Social Studies assignment.

FRED: Fuck the assignment. You killed Susan.

TRAVIS: Fred, we've been through this—

FRED: All of them. You killed all of them.

TRAVIS: The missing girls? [*He laughs.*] You think I killed the missing girls? That's crazy, Fred.

FRED: Arrest him!

TRAVIS: I didn't kill any girls.

FRED: Arrest him, Sergeant Tukovsky!

TRAVIS: Ivy, you believe me, don't you?

FRED: Don't talk to my mum! Arrest him!

TUKOVSKY: Travis, recent material has come to hand that suggests you might have some knowledge as to the whereabouts of all of the missing girls, as well as Susan Lucas.

TRAVIS: Susan Lucas?

FRED: You picked her up from the bus stop yesterday. You took her to the dunes. You fucked her there, just like you fucked Annette. Like you fucked… And now she's missing. You hurt her. I know you did.

TRAVIS: I didn't fuck Susan in the dunes.

FRED: You fucked Susan and killed her like the others. You killed my girlfriend.

TRAVIS: Hold on, could you say that louder?

He holds out the phone.

FRED: You killed my girlfriend! Arrest him, Sergeant Tukovsky!

TUKOVSKY: Travis Masters, you are to be questioned on the disappearances and possible murders of Elaine Thompson, Jessica Wren, Hilde Mueller, Annette Piggott—

FRED: And Susan Lucas.

TUKOVSKY *looks confused.*

And Susan Lucas!

IVY: Settle down, Freddo. Barry, please…

Beat.

TUKOVSKY: And Susan Lucas. You'll be questioned. When the city cops get here. [*He looks helplessly to* IVY *and* FRED.] I'm not high up enough for this.

TRAVIS *laughs and claps his hands.* TUKOVSKY *is thrown.*

What?

TRAVIS: It worked.

TUKOVSKY: What worked?

TRAVIS: I'm gonna blitz Social Studies this year. [*Beat.*] So you got an email from Susan Lucas, yes?

FRED: Yeah. Lots.

TRAVIS: And she told you if you feel threatened by me that you should take matters into your own hands. Abdomen. Lower left side.

FRED: She did.

TRAVIS: She said the police would help you out.

FRED: Yes.

TRAVIS: Pleasure to meet you face to face. Susan Lucas.

TRAVIS *holds out his hand.*

IVY: What?

TRAVIS: I'm Susan Lucas. I sent you that email. All of them, actually. From the Prefects' Room. You can check the computers in there if you like, Sergeant. I have the key.

FRED: I don't understand.

TRAVIS: It was for the assignment, Fred. 'Outback Socialisation: One Boy's Fight To Conquer Isolation'. We conquered it alright. You even fell in love.

FRED: Not with you, I didn't.

TRAVIS: Seeing as I'm Susan, it seems you did.

Beat.

FRED: Annette. You fucked Annette too. You said so. She's real. And the other missing girls. They're all in mysecret.com.

TUKOVSKY: Annette is still missing, Travis. And we know she exists.

TRAVIS: Annette is missing but she's not dead. She's pregnant. Went to Borona to get it dealt with. Didn't want her parents to know. She'll be back at the fish and chip shop in no time. And the 'secrets' you read online were all planned. All part of the assignment. I don't know anything about those missing girls, but they sure came in handy for this project. The power of suggestion is an amazing thing.

FRED: Your dad. What about your dad?

TRAVIS: My dad's on his way back from the Amalfi Coast, right Sergeant?

FRED: That's your stepdad. You killed your dad. The tractor.

TRAVIS: My dad's James Masters. I come from a good functional nuclear family, Freddo. The tractor thing was just to make you feel better about your own dad.

Beat.

IVY: You little prick.

FRED: You're Susan…

TRAVIS: Amongst others.

FRED: frida39? girlnexttdoor666?

TRAVIS: It was for the assignment. Sub-heading: 'Is a person still isolated if their friends are make-believe?'

IVY: You experimented on my little boy?

TRAVIS: You were all part of it. You gave up your own secrets so easily I couldn't help but get drawn into your sordid little web. If anyone's guilty it's you. I think the photo proves that, Ivy. I'm barely legal, for Christ's sake! What did you think of that photo, Fred? Still think I'm a fag?

FRED: I don't know what you are. [*He turns to* IVY.] Why'd you do that, Mum?

Beat. IVY *is taken aback.*

IVY: Freddo, I didn't know he'd taken that photo. I was… I'm so sorry.

FRED: Why'd you let him touch you like that? Why'd you let him do that?

IVY: I was lonely, Freddo. It's been that long since anyone showed me any kind of attention. I'm only thirty—

TRAVIS: I don't think he's talking about me, Ivy. Are you, Fred?

FRED *points to* TUKOVSKY.

FRED: Him.

Beat.

TRAVIS: He watched. While you two were doing your thing. While his dad was hanging himself from the eucalypt. Fred watched through the keyhole. Every Thursday. Like clockwork.

IVY: Fred.

FRED: [*to* TUKOVSKY] I put that huntsman in your boot.

TUKOVSKY: Fred mate…

FRED: I watched. Every Thursday. I watched.

A long beat. TRAVIS *smiles.*

TRAVIS: I'd like some time alone with Fred, Sergeant Tukovsky.

TUKOVSKY: Absolutely not. That's against all protocol.

TRAVIS: But you're not high up enough for official business, Sergeant. [*He picks up his phone and holds it high.*] Plus, I press one button on this phone and that photo of Ivy goes to everyone I know, as does an email explaining what Jim Finch really saw as he hung from that tree. Knowing Chapman, your wife should hear within the hour.

A long beat.

FRED: I'll be right, Sergeant. Mum, go with him.

TUKOVSKY *and* IVY *start to leave. At the door,* IVY *turns.*

IVY: I miss him, Fred. I just really miss him.

They leave. FRED *and* TRAVIS *are alone.*

A long moment, then…

TRAVIS: You okay?

FRED: What are you doing?

TRAVIS: It's for Social Studies, Freddo. You wanted to pass, didn't you? What's better than being the subject of a great big social experiment?

FRED: Don't bullshit me.

TRAVIS: I didn't want you to fail. Didn't want you to have to leave school.

FRED: That's not the reason.

TRAVIS: It's my job to look out for people. It's my job.

FRED: You didn't look out for me! You hurt me! I'm going to prison!

TRAVIS: I won't press charges. I just wanted to help. I just wanted to connect.

FRED: For a Social Studies assignment?

TRAVIS: No. Just for you. Bonfire Boy.

FRED: You're really sick, Travis.

TRAVIS: That's 'cause you stabbed me.

FRED: That's 'cause she told me to. Susan. You told me to.

Beat.

FRED *walks over to the bed. He slowly climbs onto it and sits astride* TRAVIS. *He takes* TRAVIS' *phone and strokes his hair.* TRAVIS *smiles.*

You're Susan?

TRAVIS: I'm Susan.

FRED: Did you mean what you said? As Susan? Did you mean it?

TRAVIS: Every word.

FRED: Why did you pretend? Why couldn't you have just said that stuff as you?

Beat.

TRAVIS: Because I knew you wouldn't want me.

A long beat. FRED *touches* TRAVIS' *eyes, his cheek, his mouth. Then his throat. He clasps his throat tightly.*

FRED: Fuck you.

TRAVIS: What?

FRED: Fuck you, you bastard.

TRAVIS: Freddo…

FRED: You lying, selfish, dirty, weak little boy.

TRAVIS: Fred…

FRED: You're the runt. You fucked my mum. You used her like they all do. Why would you do that?

TRAVIS *chokes.*

TRAVIS: You went behind my back with Susan.

FRED: You are Susan, Travis.

He tightens his grip.

Bum. Bum bum bum bum bum.

FRED *stops. Releases his grip. He stays seated on top of* TRAVIS.

TRAVIS: I wasn't always playing a part, Fred. I promise you that. I meant what I said. When you stabbed me. I meant it.

Beat.

FRED: What did you say?

TRAVIS: You don't remember?

FRED: Nope.

Beat. He gets off TRAVIS *and starts taking apart the phone.* TRAVIS' *smile fades.*

TRAVIS: You really don't remember what I said?

FRED *continues dismantling the phone.*

I said…

He looks at FRED. *Holds out his hand to him.* FRED *looks at it blankly. Beat.*

I said…

FRED *looks at* TRAVIS *for a moment then turns his back.*

TRAVIS *lowers his hand as* FRED *begins to go.*

I said…

FRED *turns back to* TRAVIS.

FRED: You have to leave me alone now.

He leaves, putting the pieces of the phone in his pocket.

TRAVIS: I said… I love you.

I lobe you.

I love you.

TRAVIS *is alone in his hospital bed. He looks small. Isolated. Demolished.*

A long beat. Then...
Case study seven...
Lights out.

THE END